LONDON UNDER FIRE
1940-45

MRS ROBERT HENREY

For the Fontbonne College
St Louis . Missouri
from
Madeleine Henrey
May 1972

LONDON
J. M. DENT & SONS LTD

Made in Great Britain
at the
Aldine Press · Letchworth · Herts
for
J. M. DENT & SONS LTD
Aldine House · Bedford Street · London

Adapted from the trilogy
A Village in Piccadilly 1942
The Incredible City 1944
The Siege of London 1946

First published in this edition 1969

SBN: 460 03906 7

CONTENTS

ILLUSTRATIONS

This shall be written for those that come after,
When London, my mother, and the other loved cities of Europe
Are praising the Lord of Life with a different skyline.
This shall serve to remind them of famous townsmen,
And monuments that war has withered like grass.

—From *Twentieth Century Psalter* by Richard Church

1940

A VILLAGE IN PICCADILLY

1940

'THREE o'clock on a November day! Piccadilly Circus was half obscured by drizzling rain and mist, and the first row of cars coming from Lower Regent Street slithered to a standstill as the lights turned from green to amber. . . .'

My husband had trained me to provide the colour of the London streets for a column we intermittently wrote for a London paper. I was less by inclination than by dutifulness a newspaper girl. Everything was wrong with my prose. I merely had a deep sorrow for other people's misfortunes. I gossiped, as my mother had done with other women in the streets where I was born. As I grew older, to find myself endowed with an essentially feminine inquisitiveness for what was in the air served a useful purpose. I never minded what happened to the colourful dust picked out of the London streets and passed on. There were these pages, for instance, from which at the beginning I tried to disassociate myself, until they kept on coming back to me. Time showed the period to have been a phase not only in my life but in the long, proud history of the greatest city in the world. I had been thrown, the most unimportant of all young women with a baby in June 1940, into a small backwater behind Piccadilly, where circumstances willed me to watch from a trembling woman's point of view, for four years, all the agony and pride of the heart of London under fire. I lived with my baby on the ground floor of a block of apartments called Carrington House in Shepherd Market. In the following pages, in compact form, stripped of the disguise which for reasons of my own I made use of at the time, is an

omnibus of the three volumes I wrote while bombs dropped
and buildings blazed, while sheet-glass windows fell on my
baby's pram: A Village in Piccadilly; The Incredible City;
The Siege of London.

THE beginning of a woman's life is divided into phases: girlhood, marriage, motherhood. Afterwards, well, that is a
matter of chance. In my case, exactly one year after having my
baby, I lost my house and garden, my dresses and shoes, all
the material things a woman collects and loves, and even the
country in which I was born!

Thus on a June morning in 1940 I arrived at the Savoy
Hotel in London with a baby, a pushcart, a feeding bottle
and a husband who had gone to France to fetch me and who
was as bewildered as I was.

The loss of all my possessions, the fact of being cut off
from the past and thrown into the bubbling waters of the
future, was to lead to something so utterly wonderful
morally that even during its most terrible moments I
rejoiced in being alive. For who in her right senses would
have missed seeing the glory that was London, London with
the enemy at its throat, London at war!

As a teenage girl I had worked at the London Savoy as a
manicurist and had only left the place to get married on
1st December 1928 at St George's, Hanover Square. After
this as a young married woman I drank champagne and
danced often on the lovely dance floor of the Savoy restaurant until the summer of 1939 when, having unwisely
bought a small farm in Normandy, I gave birth there to
my son, Bobby, remaining with my child and my mother,
naïvely believing in the Maginot Line. But the Germans
rolled across the Seine, setting fire to the countryside,
driving us before them.

From this desolation, blamed by my English parents-
in-law for not having bought a place in England instead
of in France, I arrived bemused, ashamed, frightened, in the
glittering, picturesque Strand where nobody seemed to have

any idea of the horror that was Europe, of the shrieks of women and little children machine-gunned from the air, of the imminent danger to Britain.

My pushcart was very unusual and elegant and could be folded up and carried, its aluminium frame being feather-light. With the feeding bottle I had also brought back a Scottish tartan rug. The porters of the Savoy Hotel all knew me and indeed some of them remembered not only my good days, the days, the days of my good fortune, but also those when I was the youngest employee at the barbers' shop. They saluted me smilingly and admired the baby which in my eyes was more precious than any diamond on the finger, more satisfying than a house filled with books and beautiful clothes. The baby, in spite of the immense tragedy all about me, made me feel even younger than when as a girl I worked in the hotel and so many men were in love with me.

London is always a joy to walk back into, but on this occasion London appeared fantastic in my eyes, its colour-ing so vivid that it blinded me. How elegant the women in Fortnum and Mason! How numerous the expensive cars in Piccadilly! How difficult to suppose that the fears that had shaken me only yesterday could be as terrifying as I had imagined. Were people really being machine-gunned in their cars as they drove blindly farther west towards the Atlantic? Had the once proud French army become the rabble I had seen along the roads, on the sunny sands at St Malo? Those soldiers lying with their trousers torn, their tunics open, not caring any more what happened.

I stopped in front of a furrier in Berkeley Street. The owner and his wife were charming people, suave, clever and highly civilized. The shop was divided into two parts, with two separate windows. In one part the husband sold the loveliest furs I have ever seen, the most sumptuous mink, shorn beaver (then new and very fashionable), lynx and chinchilla. In the other part the owner's wife, for whom I had great affection, sold the most glorious, hand-made, silk lingerie of a kind one never sees any more, this incredible luxury having given way to what we now wear in nylon.

Husband and wife had no illusions about the future. They were too international in outlook and experience to believe that the sort of things they sold would remain in demand for long. But I stood between one window and the other like Cinderella in my rags, dreaming, just longing to touch. Life in the country, even with the flowers blooming and the cows round one, is all very pretty, but for a young woman, even blessed with a baby, there is a drab monotony in wearing an old skirt and a pullover every day of the week. My wardrobes on the farm were full of the most gorgeous clothes, the loveliest furs, that my husband had stupidly taken over on the grounds that they would be safer there than in London. I never quite forgave him for this. I now no longer had a dress, a piece of lingerie, a coat or a handbag to my name. Everything I possessed was left behind and would be stolen.

Now I would do a little shopping. Now the world could fall apart. I must become human again. I bought a dress and the loveliest lingerie I have ever owned. The dress with the perky white collar and the midnight blue faille silk with spots was adorable. My husband was anxious to be forgiven for having taken unnecessarily so great a risk. He should not have left us there until the last moment. He should have managed in some way to have brought my mother back. He knew that in spite of my dress I was on the point of explosive tears. He would have fallen over himself to do the right thing. He took me along Lansdowne Passage and bought me the most beautiful baby male pekinese!

I called it by the absurd name of Pouffy.

Albert Gilles was then manager of the Savoy and his wife, Jeanine, lent me a cot from her own nursery which was put up at the foot of our bed. We could thus leave the baby by himself when we went out, though in fact he was seldom alone, for all the maids and the waiters on the floor used to go in every few moments to play with him. As, until the moment of our flight before the advancing Germans, he had never left the farmhouse or his native orchards, he was filled with wonderment by all this activity, and in particular by the telephone, whose novelty made him quickly forget, alas, the grandmother from whom he had been so cruelly parted.

The pekinese completed his joy. Though I temporarily had no home, I had at least a family.

This euphoria was short-lived. Albert Gilles, Londoner by adoption but Frenchman by birth and character, suddenly felt all the dishonour of his country's defeat fall upon him and this man who, at the Savoy, had received the great and the wealthy, the famous and the beautiful, would be found at the end of a corridor in tears. I fell into much the same state when, a few hours after our arrival, my youngest sister-in-law came to see us. She had not yet seen her small nephew. Her presence in this beautiful suite overlooking the Embankment Gardens and the Thames filled me with an inferiority most painful. My mother-in-law's house in Surrey where my sister-in-law lived was full of silver, of linen, of English period furniture, of rich carpets and servants. I stood in this hotel unhappy, ruined, vanquished, all that I had bought and cherished in a country over-run by the enemy about to be pillaged by my own people. Yet how much more fortunate I was than so many others. In a sense I had come home. This country, by marriage, by adoption, by the roots I had put down here, was mine.

My husband went back to the newspaper on which we both worked. I was myself being drawn back into this world in which some sort of second sense is eternally, beyond reason, beyond love, on the alert. The great hotel where during his absences I was left alone, this immensely colourful piece of London which, since the days of Gilbert and Sullivan, was always filled with politicians, film stars, business executives and theatrical folk, suddenly became hushed for the first time in half a century. It was as if some cold hand had descended upon it, chilling all it touched. Not only was the hotel, I suddenly found, practically empty, but the famous grill-room was closed so that workmen could remove the enormous glass windows facing the court-yard and replace them with a brick wall in case of air raids. The restaurant overlooking the Thames and the Embankment remained open, but its normal atmosphere had gone. The city folk who normally patronized it at lunch time, spending their money lavishly on brandy and cigars, seemed to have faded away. In place of them one met groups of Poles, Dutchmen, Belgians, Norwegians and a few American newspapermen who had just crossed over from France. General de Gaulle, almost unknown yet, held court at a large round table. French diplomats from the embassy, and members of the various naval, military, and economic missions who nearly all intended to obey the instructions of the Pétain government, kept as far from the new leader as possible, and even glared at him with undiplomatic rudeness. They intended to insist on their safe conduct home as soon as possible. There was not the slightest glamour about this international crowd. It was sombre and depressed. There were no champagne and cigars, no laughter, no long discussions over coffee, no pretty women to show off their new hats. For once the Savoy restaurant looked like the dining-room of a temperance hotel. Few people spoke above a whisper. In the big entrance hall they moved about like ghosts, shattered and bewildered by the complete and utter wreckage of their homelands.

Passing through the foyer at about five o'clock one evening I saw a dozen shabby figures walking in Indian file into the reading room. What struck me first about them was their bent and lifeless backs. They looked as if they were being led to the gallows by a member of the Gestapo. I saw them sink limply into the settees. Soon their heads were close together as they talked and argued in low tones.

Suddenly I recognized familiar faces in this little crowd. Yes, indeed, they were France's most famous war and political correspondents, men and women whose names were known throughout the world, and whom I had met personally on every great international news story since I had taken to covering such events with my husband. But what an unbelievable change had come over them! The frail, white-haired woman was Geneviève Tabouis of the Paris *Œuvre*, whom the Nazis only a few days earlier had claimed to have captured. There was Elie Bois, gruff but dynamic, brave and honest editor-in-chief of the huge circulation *Petit Parisien*; 'Pertinax', considered by the Anglo-American Press as an oracle; and Quilici of the Havas Agency, whose greatest coup had been to reveal and torpedo the Hoare-Laval plan. These writers, ever since the Versailles Peace Treaty, had moved across the continent of Europe watching revolutions, conferences, civil wars and dictators. They represented the greatest newspapers of the greatest continental power. They had caused governments to fall, and called their own cabinet ministers by their Christian names. As individuals they were much more important than our own political writers who, most unwisely, were never allowed into the confidence of Cabinet leaders. My husband had seen them in force at Lausanne when Mussolini was fresh from the triumphs of his so-called march on Rome; he had drunk beer with them at the Bavaria at Geneva where Briand and Stresemann topped the variety bill. I had met them constantly in Paris, where all of them were charming to the young woman writer so desperately looking for a way to express herself otherwise than through her husband's column.

Now they had covered the greatest story of all; but the story was too big for them and had burned them up. They no longer had any papers in which to write what they had seen; they had no longer any country to call their own. They were cut off from their families, spat on by their own government, which pillaged their homes, declared them traitors for continuing the fight and deprived them of their greatest heritage—their nationality.

They were exhausted and penniless. Their minds were reeling from incomprehension.

I went over and welcomed them, but in their mental confusion I would have done better to stay aloof. Mme Tabouis was outlawed and without news of her soldier son whom, if he was not dead already, she might never see again. Her Paris flat, filled with the treasures of a literary mind, was ransacked first by the Nazis and probably later by the French. She, whose pen wrote so fluently, could no longer put a sentence together. She tried to find words, and then sank into sobs. Elie Bois went over and over his last tragic days at Bordeaux, and kept tapping his forehead with his index finger as he cried:

'Yes, but why, why, why? There's a missing link some-where. Something we don't understand.'

A page-boy slipped into the room and turned on a radio set, from which suddenly came a strident voice announcing the terms of the armistice. The refugees, exhausted by excitement and five days' sea journey in a ship, winced at the words. The world they had known and swayed was crashing about them.

In the foyer a couple of young women with neat summer hats and flowered dresses broke into peals of laughter. Wearing my own new faille dress and light shoes I walked past them towards the cocktail bar, where a buzz of voices, a draught from an open window and billows of cigarette smoke greeted me. The room was almost gay. 'Madeleine!' somebody cried. 'Madeleine!' I turned sharply. My name was being called by young Philippe de Croisset, son of the playwright, who owed his transportation back to England to Lord Lloyd, who met him on the quay at Bordeaux. Philippe had last been in London less than a month earlier, when he was evacuated from Dunkirk. He was very young, younger than I was. I had first met his father at their beauti-ful apartment in the Boulevard St Germain. My husband had known the family at the end of the 1914–18 war when President Wilson was staying with them in their superb mansion in the Place des États-Unis during the Versailles Conference. Princess Marina's family had often been the de Croissets' guests. The roles were now reversed. Philippe was the refugee, and had just received a telephone call from the Duchess of Kent inviting him to stay over the week-end. He had brought nothing from France but a small diamond his mother had given him. He liked to think he was facing the uncertain future with this stone as his only fortune.

He was dazed by the events of the last six weeks, and by the nightmare that preceded Dunkirk. He was accompanied by a young Pole in the dark blue uniform of a French *chasseur*. The two young men insisted that I should have a drink with them. The young Pole doped his cocktail with a sleeping draught, because he told us that each time he closed his eyes he saw Nazi tanks thundering towards him.

That night we were wakened by the sirens just before midnight. It was not London's first air-raid warning, but came at a moment when people's nerves were shaken by the French débâcle and the knowledge that the Luftwaffe must soon be directed against us in all its fury. As nothing could be as bad as what I had seen in France and as I was desperately tired, I appealed to my husband, who had only just come back from the office, to let us remain where we were. Within a few moments, however, the bedside telephone rang. 'The siren has gone,' said the operator. 'Will you please go down to the shelter.' In order not to argue, I thanked him and turned over in bed, but five minutes later the telephone rang a second time, and the assistant manager gave us the same message. Ten minutes after that Mr Gilles himself rang, and almost begged me to go down. He even threatened to come and fetch us. I was not sure how much was due to his fears for our safety, and how much was prompted by his desire to inaugurate the hotel's shelter. He gave me the impression of wishing to stage a first night.

Only later did I realize to what extent his own nerves were frayed. It was obvious that we would get nowhere by obstinate resistance, so we dressed and took the child down. We found the ballroom, scene of so many brilliant banquets, shored up with steel girders, and there were bunks built between rows of damp sandbags. The wives of the senior members of the hotel staff had donned nurses' uniforms with big red crosses on their breasts, and were pouring out cups of tea for their friends in the gas-proof hospital. The orchestra from the supper-room was grouped heroically in a corner playing subdued jazz to keep up our spirits, and Bernstein, the playwright, his fine features ashen through fatigue, reclined on a bunk in a silk dressing-gown, playing the banjo.

Rey, until a short time earlier owner of The Hague's world-famed Hôtel des Indes, moved noiselessly from pillar to pillar, silently nursing his grief. His wife had been shot dead in his arms while they were motoring to the Dutch coast. I went over to him and diffidently offered him my sympathy. Some years earlier he had received us with splendid hospitality at his lovely hotel. There seemed only a faint spark of life left in him now, and he spoke in a dull, toneless voice. As soon as the Nazis invaded Holland he had discovered that many of the German guests in his hotel were fifth columnists, who became increasingly overbearing as their compatriots neared the city. Then the Gauleiter explained that he must take over the hotel, and that Rey was a prisoner. He asked permission to telephone to the local police from his room, but they were so terrified of the aggressors that they were unwilling to assert their authority. One evening Rey and his wife slipped out of the hotel and found a taxi-driver willing to drive them to the Hook, where two British destroyers were standing by. It was during this journey that his wife was shot, not by the Nazis, but by some Dutch soldiers who lost their heads. Nazi planes flying low overhead had made the soldiers nervous. The car was stopped, and Mme Rey's inert body laid at the side of the road. A Dutch officer came up and apologized clumsily for this appalling error, but said that the car must proceed immediately, and that Rey must leave his wife behind. This tragedy was sufficient to drive any man out of his wits, but Rey's suffering was not at an end. One of the British vessels was machine-gunned and sunk as he was about to go on board; the other one reached England safely, but only after a terrible journey.

Moving like a shadow amongst the sandbags in this dimly lighted shelter while the unreal sounds of the jazz band came from the tired orchestra, he made a terrible picture of human wreckage. Most of the French newspaper correspondents I had seen earlier in the evening were here also, continuing their perplexed arguments in low tones. They would soon have to leave the hotel, no longer having expenses to draw upon. Many of them, like Mme Tabouis, planned to move into cheap lodgings until they could obtain permission to leave for New York. There were also a few American journalists, convinced after what they had seen in Europe that Great Britain could never withstand the Nazi onslaught.

The next morning Londoners joked about the night's warning. No bombs had fallen, and indeed not an aeroplane was heard, but many people hearing the all clear in the early hours had mistaken it for the warning, and rushed down to their shelters. On leaving the hotel I found the Strand crowded with burly Australians and small tough Maoris who had just arrived. They threaded their way slowly in groups of three or four along the busy pavements. There were also numerous French sailors wondering what would happen to them when their ships were taken over by the British Navy. Soon they would have to choose between joining the Free French movement and being sent to camps to await repatriation. Already their officers were trying to influence them in favour of Vichy, believing our defeat inevitable. The shops were filled with peacetime plenty— scones and cakes and loaves of white bread piled on the counters of the bakers' shops; silk stockings and multi-coloured lingerie; suits at fifty shillings and poplin shirts at pre-war prices.

C. B. Cochran, the theatrical producer whose first nights before the war were legendary, met me, and said he was planning to leave the hotel and move into a flat in a great cement and steel building just off Piccadilly, and he suggested I should go and see if we also could find accommodation there. West-End flats were at a discount. People had not yet the faintest idea of what would happen when London was raided from the air, and most Londoners who had money thought the best thing was to go into the country for a few months. Those who could not spend all their time away at least made arrangements to sleep a few miles out. I had no difficulty, therefore, in finding a choice of empty flats. The most suitable was a ground-floor apartment with window boxes filled with geraniums overlooking the entrance court. From the room I planned to make my dining-room and sewing-room there was an open view of the Piccadilly sky-line because the wall on the opposite side of the courtyard was only one storey high, and covered with green trellis work to give a garden effect. The flat would surely be filled with sunshine all day long. My husband offered half the normal rental, not realizing how kind and generous the landlords later proved. Fortunately his offer was accepted and we moved in during the following week-end.

The evening papers announced the sinking of the 15,000-ton liner *Arandora Star* by an enemy submarine off the Irish coast. The loss of this ship produced a big sentimental reaction because, converted from a one-time chilled meat carrier on the Blue Star's South American route and painted a dazzling white, she was the first cruise ship to cater entirely for that class of business during the shipping crisis of the thirties, and during her life of pleasure had carried hundreds of thousands of holiday makers to sunlit lands. She had cruised in the Mediterranean, in the Norwegian fjords, and in West Indian sapphire-blue waters, and was commonly known as the 'Dream Ship'. Young and pretty enough to flirt and dance in the light of the midnight sun or under tropical skies, I had gone at various times on all these cruises. What a lovely ship she was! How I had loved her! She had become synonymous with the picturesque, happy, idle years that directly preceded the war.

No details were given of her doom, and she was dismissed as just another famous ship sent to the bottom of the sea. The next morning as I handed my key to the inquiry clerk at the Savoy, he told me he had just heard that the hotel's banqueting manager, Zavattoni, had lost his life in the ship. The implication was sensational, for if Zavattoni had been on board it was reasonable to suppose that the vessel was carrying Italians overseas for internment, and in this case there was no telling how many of London's famous *restaurateurs* had shared the same fate. I called a taxi and drove to half a dozen of the chief hotels and restaurants. Everywhere there was consternation amongst the staff, and the tragedy was clearly more complete than I had guessed. Wives were continually receiving notification of their husbands' deaths, and the list of drowned grew larger every hour. There was Maggi of the Ritz, the corpulent and jovial Benini of the Hungaria, Cavadini of the Berkeley, Boscani of Hatchetts, who was at one time in charge of catering on the *Olympic*, Zangiacomi of the Piccadilly, who had been at the hotel since 1910, and Sovrani, the great Sovrani, vice-consul of the toy state of San Marino, the impeccably dressed, diamond-front-studded arbiter of a perfect dinner, confidant of diplomats and newspaper proprietors. The death of any one of these would have hit the front page of the more popular national dailies in normal times. It is true they had become enemy aliens, but they were none the less striking characters of this cosmopolitan London of ours. Gualdi, director in its heyday of the Embassy Club, had clung for ten hours to a raft, having been wounded and shot at by his partners of the Axis.

The story was far more significant than the mere loss

of a shipload of famous London night-life figures. It drew
the curtain on a decade of West-End restaurant glamour
inaugurated by the Duke of Windsor when Prince of Wales.
The abdication, it is true, had dislodged the first stones, but
the brilliance of London after dark was sufficient to run on
for a good many years on its momentum. The restaurants
and night clubs that achieved international fame had been
crowned by the patronage of the royal brothers. This was
true of the exclusive Embassy Club in Old Bond Street,
where Edward and his brother George virtually held court
two or three times a week. It was they who had put their
stamp of recognition on Quaglino's, where the centre tables
were known as the Royal Enclosure, and were reserved for
the princes and their courtiers, who danced their way from
haunt to haunt, setting the fashion in the cut of a dinner
jacket, the choice of a buttonhole, the style of a dress, the fall
of a curl, the colour of a lipstick, the form of a *minaudière*.
My husband and I went out every evening during this
fabulous period, for we were writing columns in big circulation evening papers both in London and Paris. For me this
life was a continual joy, the sort of life that every girl dreams
of—a white ermine cloak, superb dresses my mother made
me and real diamonds in my hair! The end was the end of
my Cinderella, carefree youth (actually it had ended when I
had my baby but this put it in the irretrievable past). I
would never be so young, so full of laughter again. It was at
Quaglino's that supper society first saw the Prince of Wales
and Mrs Simpson in love, dancing cheek to cheek, oblivious
of the crowd around them. The outstanding *restaurateurs*
knew how to flatter and scheme, to fit the bill to the emin-
ence of the client (the more important he was the less he
paid), to group the *élite* and keep the public at a respectful
distance. They gave costly presents on the slightest excuse;
their caviare, their plovers' eggs, their peaches and their
nectarines were always of the choicest. Some rose to success
by being supple, others by being haughty. Sovrani, giddy
with fame, carried his mightiness to insolence. I once saw

him strut through his kingdom wearing velvet knee-breeches and decorations, bound for some official reception to which he was invited by reason of his vice-consular post. But I remembered such delightful evenings with him: in his restaurant where he liked to serve us the same superb food he had learnt to appreciate as a young man at Voisin in Paris; in his apartment where he would put on the records of Caruso; at Le Touquet where we sometimes went for week-ends and where, of course, he knew all the hotel and restaurant people who made us welcome—and treated me like a princess. They were all dressed by the most expensive tailors in Savile Row, learning to ride in the Row like the clients they served. They went away at week-ends in limousines driven by English chauffeurs. Some, like Gualdi, owned beautiful estates in Italy, where they lived for six weeks in the summer like seigneurs, but their hospitality was touching and complete.

That many were Fascists I have no doubt at all. The regime swelled them with pride. I used to find them in the early hours of the morning, when the supper rush was over, having a quick meal in a screened-off part of their restaurant discussing politics above the distant rhythmical roar of the dance band. But mostly their interests centred round royalty and the peerage, their press cuttings and the plans of their competitors. They were jealous, but considerate, gay, lavish and generous. They were symbols of an aristocracy that thought in terms of £10,000-a-year dance bands, cocktail parties, Le Touquet and Cannes.

The cracks in this edifice, visible at the time of the abdication, widened at Munich. The restaurants continued to do good business, but the clientele had changed. The Royal Enclosure was now only a memory for those who had known it, a story of Prince Charming for those who had not. During the first winter of the war every place was packed with an international medley that had flocked here from central Europe, already conquered by the Nazis. Many had moved from Vienna to Prague, from Prague to Warsaw, a move ahead of the conqueror. Night life is always at its most frenetic on the eve of a great calamity. In London also were young officers in khaki, mostly on leave from the provinces, and Frenchmen from the various missions. The Embassy Club was now a bottle party, where people drank half the night. There was nothing in common with the elegance of its regal days, when every woman's dress was a masterpiece, and Jackson, the sleek black cat, used to jump on the royal table to be stroked by two sons of a king. But money rolled into the cash desks, and the '400' was netting its owners £300 profit a week.

Italy's declaration of war had come as a shock to the Italian colony. How is it that they had never tried to escape with their money while their country was neutral? Did the thought never occur to them? Were they so steeped in English life that they could not tear themselves away from our soil, and the places they had made famous at the cost of so much hard work? They were taken away in a single night during one huge police sweep. Only a few escaped the net.

Our flat was the loveliest, the smallest, the best heated and the most comfortable I had ever known. The porters were as smart and polite as those at Claridge's (in spite of the war which was only just beginning) and the bathroom, full of mirrors, was a real joy. There was no furniture. I bought a large cherrywood dining table, three gilt chairs at an auction (the kind hired out for smart weddings) and a very broken-down armchair. We had saved our double bed— the one my mother-in-law had given me at the time of my wedding. The apartment's previous owner had left us her beautiful fitted carpets. In the bedroom, there were mirror-faced, built-in wardrobes.

Our building, just off Piccadilly, was not large enough to be impersonal, and I do not suppose that at any time there were more than a hundred people living in it. Most of the tenants owned estates in the country, and only came up to town for a few days in the middle of each week.

I liked to compare our building to a luxury liner tied up at the quay of a small port. There was a Diesel room below (for the central heating), and a corridor flanked with stout pipes for water and oil which increased this marine atmosphere. The back door was on a lower level than the front entrance, and by going down a short flight of steps we could therefore take this corridor to lead us out into the small streets. We were practically self-contained. The company had its own carpenters, glaziers, electricians and plumbers. There were valets and maids equipped with electric sweepers of the most modern kind. There were two lifts, one on either side of the main entrance hall, and a passage on the sixth floor built like the covered promenade deck of a liner, with glass partitions leading out on a wide roof garden, from which one could look down on the surrounding houses much smaller than our own. The view was so admirable that I doubt if any other building apart from the Dorchester or the Air Ministry in Berkeley Square could give a more magnificent sweep over the roofs and spires of London.

We towered over Shepherd Market—that village sleepily living its own life just behind Piccadilly. We dominated it, almost overpowered it with brute strength, for it was no larger than a handkerchief. But the contours of the market are sharply defined, and it has a vigorous character. From the top of our roof we could look down on Shepherd Street, the market's main street, which runs into the market-place proper with its butcher's shop, its fishmonger, its greengrocer, the oil and candle store and its public-houses. In those days the normal way of entering the market from Curzon Street, the northern boundary, would have been under covered passages built between low, squat houses at least two centuries old which, in summer, were picturesque because of the geraniums in boxes on every sill. Tourists came to drink sherry in the Free Vintner's bar. They bought coloured postcards of the market to send home, thinking it queer that there was so much local colour so near to the throb of Piccadilly.

ONE Sunday in July at a small Georgian house in Bedford Square we met a French naval officer, his right foot swathed in cotton wool and bandages, who dominated the conversation after lunch. This man had a spell-binding personality. He was tall, slim, with deep black eyes, the hooked nose of a bird of prey and a weather-beaten face which made him look considerably older than his twenty-nine years. He was a Vendean, of noble but piratical blood, perfectly expressed in his name—le capitaine de vaisseau de la Porte des Vaux.

At the age of nineteen, so he told us, he had already travelled twice round the world. During three weeks of this fateful summer he was torpedoed twice, once in Norwegian waters, the second time at Dunkirk. He then led his men on shore and fought the Nazis with Mills bombs and revolvers, which cost him a fractured foot, a shattered collar-bone and a broken leg. He was enthusiastic because he had been given command of a ship under the Free French flag.

I saw a good deal of him while he was waiting to put out to sea, and the more I saw him, the more he struck me as a modern Robert Surcouf. He had inherited the corsair's distrust of the English (for did we not drive those Frenchmen off the high seas?), but he declared that as the British were eager to go on killing Germans he was delighted to continue doing so in our company. He said he had his views on Marshal Pétain, but on principle he would punch the nose of any Englishman who insulted him, for Pétain was a Marshal of France and Head of the State, and only history could tell if he was working against us.

The captain did not spend all his time in London. He used to travel down to the port where his ship was making ready to put to sea; but his impetuous nature nearly sent him to jail. One evening, when a local taxi-driver refused to drive him from the station to the quay because the air-raid sirens had gone, the captain dug his revolver into the cabby's ribs, succeeding by force where he had failed by persuasion. The Board of Admiralty solemnly discussed this breach of naval etiquette, but all apparently ended well.

He composed a flamboyant order of the day addressed to his crew which he read out to us:

'Tomorrow I shall lead you into battle. The aim of this fight is to show the world that France, in standing by her promise to continue the struggle, retains her honour and her flag. We shall be nameless and free from party politics. We are simply acquitting a debt to our country by sacrificing everything to her, even our families, in return for the thousand years of happiness and security she has given to our forefathers.'

He went off with his ship to Dakar. I suppose that it was natural for so many of the fantastic stories of the period to turn on the French débâcle. A few weeks later, for instance, I was invited to dinner in a West End hotel by a man who the same evening had communicated his own obituary to *The Times*. He introduced himself in the foyer as Mr 'James', and during the early part of the meal showed himself discreet and uncommunicative. Over coffee he became more talkative, and described how he had escaped to this country.

So determined was he to join de Gaulle that he drove to a French port without time to change into civilian clothes, and ran up the quay to the gangway of a British ship that was evacuating our last nationals from French soil. He knew that the harbour officials would prevent a French officer from going on board, and because of this he decided to stun with the butt of his revolver the first man who tried to stop him. Having carried into effect this energetic measure he scrambled on board during the mêlée that ensued, and hid himself on a lower deck till the vessel was at sea. Our immigration authorities at the port of landing proved sympathetic and he was soon at liberty. But now this unfortunate man was tortured by fears for his wife,

whom he was obliged to leave behind. She was Swiss by
birth and it had been arranged between them that he would
announce his death as soon as he reached safety, in order
that she might reclaim her Swiss nationality and then seek,
as a neutral, to join him either in England or elsewhere.

The day following our supper-party, I saw a man who
strangely resembled my host of the previous night. He had
dyed his grey hair flaxen, cut off his moustaches and bought
himself a pair of wide-rimmed tortoise-shell spectacles, but
in the brilliant sunshine the disguise was not quite perfect.

As I passed him, he drew himself up and muttered: 'The
man you dined with last night is dead.'

I had not as yet discovered the joys of the Green Park.
That was to come later. For the time being, while I was
trying to organize some sort of home life in our new apartment, I took my baby and the pekinese every afternoon to
the Daisy Walk in Hyde Park. The weather was still fine
and I could sit in a deck-chair and knit or sew, and occasionally gossip with other young mothers.

The Daisy Walk ran beside the fine undulating lawn that
is bordered by the Row and the Dell where the rabbit
warrens were. Before the war it had become the rendezvous
of smart nurses and their young charges, and photographers
used to take pictures of the babies for the society weeklies.
Only a few children remained, and their perambulators did
not bear coronets embroidered on the coverlets, but there
was little Gay, aged two years and a month, the daughter of
an actress who was a volunteer driver of a Chelsea ambulance. Gay, a sweet child with wondering eyes, had been
brought back to London from Kent with her nurse because
they had been twice bombed in the depths of the country.
These were the days of fierce aerial battles on the south-east
coast. No bombs had yet fallen on the West End. Indeed,
big wagers had been laid in clubs on the day that war was
declared that no bombs would fall for a year on the C police
division of London, and it seemed just possible that these

Bobby at the window

Below was our village

bets would be won. There were twenty-four plays and musicals in central London—four times as many as in New York City; and in spite of the incessant alerts I remember looking out of the window of our apartment one afternoon to see a carriage and pair swing into the courtyard. The sight of this shining carriage drawn by two splendid bays seemed almost unreal in a London that only a few minutes earlier had been sheltering from enemy raiders. Our hall porters had by then been issued with tin hats and hatchets, and three of these fellows hurried forward to meet the carriage. One of them, whom we called 'Hammersmith' because he lived in an Anderson shelter there, looked, in this accoutrement, like Don Quixote. He was slight of build, wore steel-rimmed spectacles, and his tin hat, much too large for him, toppled over his eyes each time he made a sudden movement. He was an incredible picture as he raced towards this fine equipage. Lord and Lady Portsea had come to pay a leisurely call on our neighbour, Mrs Elinor Glyn. Lord Portsea and the famous red-haired novelist had played together as children on the sandy beaches of the island of Jersey.

On Saturday afternoon, 7th September, my husband had come with me to the Daisy Walk.

Autumn had come to the park; lawns and paths were covered by curled-up brown leaves, but the heat was still reminiscent of mid June.

There was a fair crowd, and the brown-coated chair seller claimed to be doing even better than in normal years, for there were still many Australian and Canadian soldiers with spare time on their hands.

Our baby was just beginning to walk, and we watched him making his first steps accompanied by his faithful Pouffy. It was tea time and Londoners lying lazily under the big trees on the lawn were just unpacking thermos flasks and sandwiches from baskets.

The sirens wailed, first in the distance, and then nearer, but although a few people were hurried away by a desire to be on the move as soon as a raid was signalled, most of us took no notice. There had been so many occasions on which nothing had been seen or heard.

Then came the drone of aeroplanes which could be seen to the east at an immense height, no larger than pinheads. One needed to adjust one's eyes to the light in order to catch glimpses of the silver dots in the sky flashing at one moment in the sun, then disappearing as they banked and turned.

As more aeroplanes arrived the puffs of anti-aircraft fire appeared like little flakes of cotton wool amongst the formations. Fascinated, we watched all this for nearly an hour, but suddenly, with a deafening screech, big guns quite near us spat their metal into the sky.

I seized the child and the dog and discovered that by now we were almost alone on the lawn. Knowing that each morning the Daisy Walk was strewn with shrapnel I feared these guns more than the raiders, and we beat a precipitate retreat into Knightsbridge.

It was not until dusk, when the great fires of dockland reddened the sky, that most people realized the battle for London had started in earnest, and that the silver specks we had watched at tea time had been fighting for the mastery of the capital. The day raiders had gone home by six after dropping bombs on Woolwich Arsenal, on the gasworks at Beckton, on the docks at Millwall, on the docks at Limehouse and by Tower Bridge; at Rotherhithe, on the Surrey docks and on the West Ham power station. At ten past eight exactly the night raiders appeared, and by then the docks on both sides of the Thames were blazing furiously.

All that night the sinister glow deepened under the enemy's ruthless bombing, and only paled before the slowly approaching dawn.

We had been unwilling from the start to evacuate Bobby, who during the early part of the summer had slept unconcernedly through some of the worst bombing in France, but I was now conscious of our good fortune in having chosen a flat in so modern a building.

For a short time I continued to take Bobby to the Daisy Walk, but each day it became more deserted. The chair man now dragged his weary feet from lawn to lawn with only a few coppers in his leather satchel. Little Gay remained for a week until her parents' home, too close to Victoria station and Ebury Bridge, became untenable. Then she and her nurse disappeared.

At this point, left increasingly on my own, my husband busy, no woman friend in whom to confide, I began going to the Green Park.

To begin with it was nearer, and secondly I discovered that there was one other child who remained faithful to our London parks. He was Alexander, King Zog's son and heir, who was born just before Italy's invasion of Albania. Queen Geraldine, whose life was not then out of danger, was obliged to flee for safety across the mountains to Greece. The family now lived at the Ritz, and every day the heir to this uncertain kingdom was wheeled out in a cream-coloured perambulator by a Swiss nurse, accompanied by five swarthy male attendants whom at first I took to be plain-clothes policemen. Soon I discovered that they were all of princely rank, the flower of Albanian nobility, who had constituted themselves a guard of honour to this baby prince with flaxen silky locks and a little Lord Fauntleroy ermine coat with bonnet to match and long white leggings.

The prince had already an incipient knowledge of Albanian, French and English. Strangers were charmed by the way he piped out a regal 'bye bye' from the top of his pram as if he was already a king in a gold coach.

When Queen Geraldine wheeled the pram her courtiers followed at a discreet distance; when she sat down they drew up chairs ten paces behind. Only my unrespectful commoner son occasionally broke such strict etiquette by stealing behind Her Majesty's deck chair and calling out 'Cuckoo!'

At night Alexander and his nurse slept in a curtained-off

section of a ground-floor public room at the hotel. If, during the day, they were caught in the park when the sirens went they had strict orders to return with all haste to the Ritz. We used to watch this caravan scuttling across the park while the king and queen watched anxiously from their apartment window.

The only other child I met in the parks this winter was a little boy wheeled in a cheap pram by a bare-headed coster with a splendid crop of thick hair, worn shoes, and a green open-necked shirt. As the child grew up the pram was discarded, and father and son crossed the park slowly hand in hand. Not even the park keepers or the police ever got a word out of them. They were silent and mysterious, subjects for a novelist. Had the mother been killed in an air raid? Was this apparently speechless child dumb? On the rare occasions when he ventured a little distance from his father and was persuaded to accept a sweet, only his large eyes gave delighted thanks. He was never heard to say a word.

As the battle for London continued the face of the West End changed; but as far as possible its inhabitants attempted to carry on as usual. Crowds filed through the streets an hour before dusk carrying their mattresses on their way to the tube stations and public shelters; the restaurants began to empty, except those like the Hungaria and the Dorchester, which increased their business because of the stoutness of their construction and the fact that they allowed their supper clients to doss down for the rest of the night on improvised beds.

Bombs fell by day as well as by night. We became accustomed to the sudden drone of an aeroplane in the middle of the morning, the screech of a bomb, the dull crash of its explosion and the smell of cordite that filled the air a moment later. The sight of a burned-out bus unexpectedly in Berkeley Square, the ruins of a shop still half-hidden in a cloud of dust, streets that were impassable because of time bombs, enemy planes that burst in mid air sending down large chunks of fuselage, the pilots gliding down with their parachutes, became the normal things of life. Our shop-keepers were bad-tempered because of their incredible suffering during the long nights, but somebody would crack a joke and life seemed good again.

People continued to invite their friends to dinner, but many guests said, like Surtees's Jorrocks: 'I sleeps where I eats.'

We had decided for the sake of the child to continue our lives as normally as possible. His cot was in a corner of our bedroom, and we slept with the windows wide open without once going into a shelter. Many people looked at me askance for thus exposing the child's life, but he grew plump and rosy-cheeked, oblivious of the thuds that woke us from time to time. Our section was, according to statistics, one of the most heavily bombed in Westminster, and each morning it became a rite to visit neighbouring damage by the pale grey light of dawn. The road squads were still sweeping away the broken glass, and the hose-pipes of the Auxiliary Fire Service lay snake-like from pavement to pavement. 'We've been blown up,' said a notice outside Punch's Club. 'Will members please blow into the club next door?' A large private residence down the street was cut open, making it look like a sectional doll's house. Passers-by could see into all the rooms—the bathroom on the third floor was all ready for somebody to take a bath, with a towel lying across the metal rail. Almost every night some landmark near us would go up in dust, and yet our building continued to stand with every pane of glass regularly cleaned by the company's staff.

By mid October it was becoming more and more difficult to give my son his daily airing because the parks were closed for two or three days at a time owing to the presence of un-exploded bombs. I took him round the village and the neighbouring streets each morning, while I did my shop-ping. His hair was as golden and as curly as when we had brought him back from Normandy, and I pushed him around in his streamlined duralumin carriage very low on its wheels and fitted with mudguards which made people look twice at this turn-out, especially as Pouffy the pekinese lay curled up on the coverlet. 'The child who would not be evacuated' became a local character, and was adopted by our village, who considered him as a mascot. He was watched over with sympathetic part-ownership, and often when my husband jumped off a bus in Piccadilly on his return from the office he was given news of his movements by people he did not even know by name.

One Saturday morning, as my husband was working at home, an enemy plane, which must have momentarily cut its engines out, zoomed over the house-tops and released a bomb that crashed a few hundred yards away. The building rocked, there was a crash of broken glass, and the air was filled with a pungent smell. Knowing that I had taken the baby out shopping, he leapt through the window and hurried across the courtyard into the market. The bomb had fallen slantwise on the lower floors of a giant steel and concrete building just outside the limits of our village, and terribly mutilated bodies were already being lined up outside a public house. Blast had, as usual, left many windows nearest the explosion untouched; others inside the market were shattered. But there was no sign of us. For a moment he stood in the market hesitating which way to turn. Then the butcher and the greengrocer ran out from their shops and exclaimed: 'Don't worry, they went home by the back door a moment ago.'

The following week Leicester Square had its first big night raid, and the Naval and Military Club in Piccadilly was sliced in half. The bottle parties, however, tired of inactivity, started to re-open at 10 p.m. instead of at midnight. My women friends and I all began to buy silk stockings in quantity, fearing a shortage. Londoners saw Manchester and Birmingham buses on their streets, and our newspaper vans were obliged to make wide detours to reach the railroad termini because so many streets were closed. Some of these van drivers had curious stories to tell.

One described how he had suddenly come across the familiar notice, 'Danger—Unexploded Bomb' in the middle of the road. He stopped dead with a screech of brakes, and was wrenching his van round to take another turning when he saw a lorry hurtling in his direction. 'Hey, mate,' he cried out, 'there's a time bomb down there!' 'Don't worry,' came the answer, 'we've come to take it away,' and the bomb-removal squad sped on.

During November, while finishing the manuscript of *A Farm in Normandy*, I worked till one o'clock each morning, and then went to bed ready to sleep through anything. Just before two o'clock one morning my husband and I were wakened by the sound of an explosion a few streets away, followed by another much nearer. We held our breaths expecting a third, because that is how they so often seemed to fall—nearer and nearer. It came screeching down, finishing up with a crisp, angry, tearing punch, accompanied by a blinding flash as the building rocked and everything in the room crashed about our heads. There was a suffocating stench, a moment's complete silence, and then an imperative voice from somewhere in the night. We made a dive for the cot, found the baby intact and still asleep, and proceeded cautiously to assess the damage. It was not possible to strike a light because our windows were gaping open with the curtains wrenched off, but by a miracle the glass was not broken, probably because the air had been able to rush right in. In the adjoining room, however, where the windows had been closed, all of them were smashed, and the glass pounded to shreds and driven like nails into the opposite walls. Myriads of sharp pieces were embedded in the plaster. The pekinese was wailing, and the chairs had been torn to pieces, with their legs thrown in all directions so that we were continually tripping up over broken objects on our way into the kitchen, where it was safe to light a lamp. We dressed hurriedly, chilled by a cold November wind blowing through the flat, and wheeled the cot over a sea of broken glass into the passage where the porters were running along with lanterns, the electric light having failed. The entrance hall where we took refuge was soon filled with phantom figures difficult to recognize in the semi-obscurity. Wardens and police tramped past with their thick boots, women clad in the strangest garb fired shrill questions at the porters, who reassured them with respectful annoyance. The bomb had fallen on a garage at the corner of our court-yard, exactly opposite the drawing-room, but our building, though buffeted, stood proud and true. Nearly every window of its seven storeys had, however, crashed into the courtyard, where the glass lay a couple of feet deep. Many doors were wrenched from their frames, and there was some serious damage in the corner nearest the explosion, but nobody had been killed, though several were treated for cuts and minor injuries.

Reports came in that the Carlton Hotel had received a direct hit, and that Gelardi, the veteran manager who shortly before the war had returned from the Waldorf Astoria in New York, was somewhat seriously wounded. Just before dawn I went round to the Ritz, where I discovered that Gelardi had in fact been brought there with multiple arm injuries, and that one of the company's directors who had been living at the Carlton had gone to hospital with his wife, who was to have a leg amputated. She had been crushed between two bed frames.

I found the Carlton a scene of ghastly desolation in the light of fierce fires raging in Trafalgar Square. This hotel, which was the personification of the Edwardian period, had a lounge which led by way of half a dozen wide steps to its large and dignified restaurant. There were interior balconies above the lounge, Spanish fashion, the sills decorated with flowers. This atmosphere called for the valse rather than the foxtrot, the tango in preference to the blues. Its waiters were servitors of the school of dignified courtesy, and one had the impression that they had grown up with the place. During the hectic twenties the Carlton had refused to be jostled, and nothing was ever able to sweep away the mutton-chop-sleeve, tight-waist, pre-1914 atmosphere. This was the home of Escoffier, who was sent for by Foch after an historic dinner, during the marshal's London visit after the Armistice. The military-gastronomic combination persisted. During the first winter of the war the ill-fated Supreme War Council ate frequently here after its catastrophic meetings, and Chamberlain, Gamelin and Daladier posed for press photographers after coffee.

All this had gone up in acrid smoke. As I peered into what, a few hours earlier, had been the lounge, there was nothing to be seen but charred rafters and firemen's hoses.

I came back as the streets were just becoming light. This was the hour to see London's scars, for no roads were yet barred, no stricken-down building roped off.

The bomb that had fallen on our garage had made a sorry sight of our village street. It had shattered every window, and filled the glass-strewn road with wares of all descriptions. One was obliged to tread carefully over boxes of sardines from the general store and bottles of perfumes from the ladies' hairdressing establishment run by our local chief warden. But the queerest assortment of goods was pitch-forked into the centre of the road from the old curiosity shop run by a gentleman of eighty-nine who had a patriarchal white beard. There were officers' leggings and stage swords that had once flashed on the boards of Drury Lane in epic melodramas, women's white boots that buttoned up the side, billiard balls and telescopes and South American riding saddles. A policeman had picked up from the gutter a collection of African spears, with which he was gesticulating in the light of dawn. The greengrocer, who only two days before had put in a new window because the old one was cracked, looked disconsolately at a case of oranges that had been hurled through the plate glass and now lay disembowelled in the gutter. The public-house that faced our back entrance was blasted, and its sign, a Toby jug, hung crazily from a thread.

Mayfair's oldest house, on which was written, 'The

Cottage, 1618 A.D.' over an oak postern gate from which hung a brass lantern, was smashed like a match-box crushed under heel, and its James I rafters lay on a pile of rubble in its tiny garden, where a jackdaw's wicker-work cage hung upside down from a broken bough.

The house which was once a shepherd's cottage when all around were fields had collapsed when a bomb struck a public house opposite, killing a barmaid who had sheltered under a billiard table in the cellar. Bedrooms on the second floor were almost undamaged.

Fire bombs had fallen on a group of old buildings where clever craftsmen made trunks and other leather goods. There was a little hunchback whose work I had particularly admired when passing by a week earlier.

On that occasion also I saw a woman sketching this picturesque corner. She was seated on a low stool on the cobbled street in front of her easel, while a black cat sat solemnly beside her inspecting her picture. 'You never know,' she had said as I approached, 'all this might disappear one day.'

A crowd of Belgian navvies were brought to clear this debris away in due course, and for more than a month one heard nothing but Flemish in this part of our village.

On my return to the main street I went to the grocer who told me that nothing could be sold until the inspector from the Ministry of Food had called to condemn any food that might be contaminated with broken glass. I decided to buy some oranges and bananas that were well protected by their skins. It was not until January that these precious fruits became for many months but a memory of the past.

It was sunny but bitterly cold and as the windows of the living-room were completely smashed I knitted warm woollies for Bobby and even a coat for Pouffy! Curiously enough, our kitchen alone had suffered no damage. In the early raids we had often performed a nightly comedy of rushing into the kitchen each time we heard a bomb dropping near, on the theory that it was the best-protected spot in our flat. One morning, however, I was tempted to put

my head out of the window into the dark well in the centre
of the building, and I discovered that instead of there being
seven storeys above the ceiling there was actually nothing
at all. Thenceforth we reversed the process, diving out of
the kitchen each time that a bomb whistled down.

Our building was repaired with an efficiency that was
worthy of its high traditions. Glaziers arrived on the Sunday
morning to ply their new trade, that of fitting into the
empty casements sheets of a black tarred substance which,
though keeping out the light, protected us from the wind
and the rain. The villagers boarded up their shop windows,
later improving this temporary measure by cutting apertures
in the centre for cellophane windows, behind which they
placed a few typical goods to attract customers and show the
nature of their wares. The hairdresser displayed a single
bottle of perfume, the grocer a packet of tea and a plate of
dried fruit. Later still the more artistically inclined painted
pictures on the woodwork.

For a week we were without water, for a month without
gas, and for nearly six weeks our telephone was dead. Each
morning the porters brought up a jug of water with which
we washed and did the cooking. It was impossible to buy
electrical equipment but neighbours came to our help,
lending us electric kettles and pans. I also did my best to
fry eggs on the smooth surface of an electric iron.

Christmas brought us a bombing truce and because it was
Bobby's first Christmas in London, indeed only his second
all told, I bought a small tree and decorated it for him, and
it was lovely to feel that we were all together, my husband,
the child and Pouffy, my pekinese who had become a sweet,
intelligent and affectionate member of the family. But all
this, restful and delightful as it was, proved a nervous and
subdued respite. There was something unreal about our
nocturnal peace, and we could not help but notice that more
and more people were leaving town.

From the very first night of the battle for London, because

of the fires in the east which lit up the dome, St Paul's Cathedral had become a symbol of London's defiance. As long ago as the night of the 12th September a large delayed-action bomb hurtled down south of the granite posts and buried itself twenty-seven feet deep. Everybody knew that if it exploded there would be nothing left of St Paul's. For three days men worked to dig it out. Then it was driven in state to Hackney Marshes on a lorry under the command of Lt Davies, a Canadian who became a national hero.

Even for a very ordinary housewife living with her baby in the West End St Paul's could never for long be out of her mind. Almost every evening from the flat roof of Carrington House we peered east and prayed that it might stand.

Though personally I seldom went to the City, my husband lunched once, sometimes twice, a week at New Court in St Swithin's Lane. The previous night, the historic 29th December 1940, I had myself from the roof of our giant building watched the cathedral silhouetted against the red night sky while everything round was crackling and falling. St Paul's during that night provided the most inspiring and terrifying sight that Londoners had ever seen. At times the dome seemed to ride the waves like a galleon, and the golden cross to scintillate above the reach of earthly harm. Meanwhile at about 7.30 p.m. the south-westerly breeze which, at the beginning of the raid, was only slight, had increased to gale force, and sparks from neighbouring buildings fell in showers over the church of St Lawrence Jewry, whose predecessor was burned down in the fire of 1666. Moments later the wind was carrying fragments of burning wood towards Guildhall, and the Great Hall, the walls of which survived the fire of 1666, received red-hot embers.

As the following morning I was going with my husband to New Court, having made arrangements with the maid to look after Bobby and Pouffy, we set off rather earlier than usual. But though we were full of apprehension, not

having slept a moment all night for fear of what we would
find, I had not imagined anything like the desolation which
met us as soon as we reached the Ludgate Circus end of
Fleet Street. Progress was impossible except on foot, and
then only if one was prepared to make a wide detour through
streets littered with burning rubble and oozing with water.
To reach the vicinity of the Bank we were obliged to turn
up Farringdon Street, pass under Holborn Viaduct, skirt
round Smithfield and find a way through Gresham Street
into Cheapside. St Paul's Cathedral, as if under divine protection, stood intact, but Paternoster Row, narrow picturesque home of publishers, had by then almost burned itself
out, while new fires were starting in scores of buildings
all around. The entire area between St Paul's and Guildhall
was impassable. Firemen's hoses lay like snakes across the
streets, and from time to time an ambulance would find a
way across the debris to take some injured fireman to
hospital. The conflagration round Fore Street had been
abandoned to burn itself out, and what we were witnessing
was to prove the largest area of continuous air-raid desolation in Britain.

St Swithin's Lane, that short and extremely narrow road
that runs between the Royal Exchange and Cannon Street,
was trodden in Napoleonic times by a short man, with an
almost round face, a slightly Judaically pouting lower lip,
laughing eyes, and tufts of curly hair on either side of his
otherwise bald head, a man as legendary as the Iron Duke
himself, the financier who beat the rest of the world with
the result of the Battle of Waterloo—N. M. Rothschild Esq.
The famous red shield with its five arrows jutting out into
the narrow street outside New Court had been removed at
the beginning of the Battle of London, but within the bank
were still all the historic links with the days when the
partners' illustrious forbear financed the Duke of Wellington's Spanish campaigns.

On this nightmare morning, because of a bomb that had
fallen on one side of the street so that there was nothing but

smouldering ruins in the carriageway, it was not possible to enter the bank by its beautiful courtyard, and the side entrance had to be used. The historic building remained standing by a miracle though most of the windows were broken and all the smells of the street, burnt paper, charred wood, a damp mustiness and a white winter fog rolling up from the Thames, came through the casings.

Mr Anthony de Rothschild lunched almost every day in a room where fine oil paintings of the family through its many generations embellished the walls, and where a merry fire burned in an old-fashioned grate. Well-groomed footmen, who had known the partners since childhood, silently passed round dishes while eminent people discussed politics and foreign affairs with the moderation expected of men in high positions.

On this occasion the steps were covered with broken glass and a messenger, wearing a top-hat and carrying a rolled-up umbrella, was brushing the dust from his coat. Mr Anthony led his guests to a small room below stairs where he often slept during the air raids and where the house-keeper served them with cold tongue and chutney. There was no coffee because the gas was cut off. This perhaps was to prove one of the strangest lunches served at New Court since Napoleonic times. Once again a whole era was about to change.

1941

Margaret with Bobby in his pram

Dawn after the raid

The great fire in our village, by Winifred Berry

Shepherd Market in 1903, by an unknown artist

1941

THE New Year saw an extraordinary friendship and comprehension developing amongst the people in our village. West-End night life, also, made a pretence of gaiety, especially in places still considered safe.

It was not until early March, when the raids had started again with redoubled fury, that the final blow was struck against the London pre-war entertainment world.

One Saturday evening Martin Poulsen looked with satisfaction at his crowded Café de Paris. The café was a circular room with a balcony all round. The place was below street level, and was reached by a flight of steps leading down from the entrance in Coventry Street, almost half way between Piccadilly Circus and Leicester Square. For many years before the war the Café de Paris had alternated between being extremely smart and exclusive and catering to a much more humble clientele.

This had depended on the whims of Poulsen, a jovial but astute hard-headed Dane, and his partner Stocco, a highly strung Italian, who once won a fortune in the Irish sweepstake, a success which turned him into a nervous wreck.

Luigi, creator of the superlatively exclusive Embassy Club, brought Poulsen to the West End just after the Great War to be the club's assistant manager, but Poulsen dreamed of running places himself. He launched the Kit Cat Club in the profligate twenties, and after its bankruptcy brought to the café, which he had also acquired, artists like Raquel Meller, Lucienne Boyer, Beatrice Lillie and the Yacht Club Boys at fees which ran up as high as £600 a week. His openings were social events drawing the then King and Queen when they were Duke and Duchess of York, the Duke of Windsor when he was Prince of Wales, and the Duke of Kent when Prince George. After the novelty of an artist had worn off, or when there was no artist at all, prices dropped, and so did the quality of the café's clients. Meanwhile Martin Poulsen wanted to extend his kingdom still further. With Jack Harris, the band leader, and Aaronson, Harris's financially minded American saxophonist, Poulsen opened the '400', a bottle party for the smart set. He became manager of the London Casino, and when, just before the war, the Embassy Club fell on bad days, he realized his life's ambition by buying it up. As there was no longer any room for a club of this exclusive nature he turned it into a bottle party, being careful to make it the complement and not the competitor of the '400', which was doing such amazing business.

When the Italian colony, including his own partner, Stocco, was rounded up, Martin Poulsen suddenly found himself undisputed king of West-End night life. Thus proud, smiling and immaculate, with a red carnation in his buttonhole, did he stand in the middle of his Café de Paris on this Saturday night. The restaurant was advertised as 'the safest place to dance in Town'. Most people believed it because any basement gives a false sense of security, but in this case there was a weak spot in the form of an air shaft running from top to bottom of the building, through which by a million to one chance fell a high-explosive bomb. The orchestra was playing a foxtrot at the time, and the dance floor was crowded. There was a blinding flash, followed by a dreadful darkness, in which cries and moans could be heard. A waiter who escaped from this hecatomb said to me afterwards: 'I don't remember being frightened. It happened too quickly.' He groped his way to the balcony, where he found Poulsen and the Swiss restaurant manager, Charles, 'lying side by side like a knife and fork'. Those words were his own, and were the spontaneous description of a man used to laying the silver on a dinner table. The

Dane and the Swiss were struck down as they talked to a client. Death had come in a split second.

Our village was not the only place where Flemish was to be heard.

On Sunday mornings we used to go into Hyde Park, where an immense dump of old bricks, wood, and scrap iron was being made from sites cleared of bomb debris. It was a cemetery of iron bedsteads, burned-out motor-cars, lorries, baths, gas cookers, electric stoves, geysers, water tanks, and all the other things that are mute witnesses of domestic anguish after the raiders have passed.

Exile had not changed the habits of these Belgian navvies, who sang good-humouredly at their work, breaking off from time to time to take deep draughts from bottles of red wine.

Next to this junk shop the Office of Works, in conjunction with the Westminster City Council, had laid out several dozen allotments, so that any citizens disposed to pay a small yearly fee might grow vegetables. The earth was rich and heavy to turn, but the shortage of onions all through the winter had taught people to appreciate things they had hitherto taken for granted. Entire families arrived on Sunday mornings armed with spades and forks, and even trowels for the youngsters, to dig and plan, and dream of beans and carrots and lettuces. Seeds were planted and cotton thread run criss-cross to keep the cheeky London sparrows and fat pigeons from the tender shoots when and if they should appear.

Some of the enthusiasts went as far as the dump to offer cigarettes to the Belgians, hoping to obtain a little raw material for building glass frames. They could be seen making brave efforts to explain their needs—some wood, a few nails, and the loan of something to serve as a hammer, a few sheets of broken glass to keep the seedlings warm and out of danger. It was understood that only vegetables were to be grown on these strips of black soil, but most allotment

holders could not resist sowing a few flowers between the
runner beans and the lettuces to take home for the parlour
window.

Across the Serpentine auxiliary firemen warmed up their
motors and unreeled their hoses for a little practice. Water
was pumped out of the Serpentine, and sent back into it by
cascades that caught the sun, producing all the colours of
the rainbow. The ducks and the swans fussed and called to
one another, but never swam far from the edge because of
the great chunks of white bread that housewives, unaware
of Europe's starvation, were so prodigal as to throw
away.

For some weeks there had been a lot of mysterious coming
and going on the crocus mound above the Daisy Walk.
Information on the subject was guarded, confidential and
utterly unreliable. The gardeners and the old man with the
pony cart, who had worked in the parks for half a century,
suggested that a particularly big bomb must have fallen
there or that it was, on the contrary, a very small one that
had burrowed its way mole-like under the turf.

At all events a squad of experts arrived to camp like
Indians on the crocus mound, where they proceeded to
erect a tripod, and sink a well down which each man took
his turn to be lowered in a bucket.

Our main concern was that the Daisy Walk was put out of
bounds with red notices on the paths leading to it, warning
the public to keep away. The rabbits in the Dell became
wild again with no humans peering over the railings. Even
Knightsbridge was closed for a short time. A bomb had
been discovered under the lounge of the Hyde Park Hotel.
It had lain there for several months, powerful enough to
blow the place sky-high. Famous men had walked over it
on their way to lunch, people had danced above it. The discovery of this horrible thing was as romantic as the tracking
down of a murderer in a detective story. There were all the
elements of mysterious drama: the taxi-driver with the long
unkempt moustaches, whose cab was hurled right across the

street by an explosion, but who gave such unreliable evidence; the policeman on duty; the warden who had a 'hunch' that proved right in the end; a lecture in quite another part of London, where a man sitting quietly at the back of the hall suddenly solved the riddle.

It was only now that our village made any determined effort to band together and form a fire-fighting unit. There were difficulties, of course. With a few exceptions, like Andrey the newsagent, few of our shopkeepers lived in the community. They came in the early morning, took possession of our little republic, and disappeared at night nobody quite knew where. After dusk our village was handed over to the publicans, the night-club proprietors, the Italian café-bar owners, and to the tenants of our block of flats.

Our building was now to be turned into a watch tower, from the top of which we could survey the helpless little houses below. There would be a telephone from the 'promenade deck' down to the basement, where a rota of fire-fighters would be waiting to dash out fully equipped with all the necessary implements. Meanwhile a list of our tenants was examined to discover how many would be willing or able to do such service once a week on the roof. It turned out that most of them were too old, others said they were absent most of the week, and yet others had weak hearts or were civil servants, which appeared to exclude them from any fire-watching other than at their own offices. My husband ended by collecting about two dozen volunteers, most of whom were women. One was a German maid, who claimed some relationship to the Nazi general Milch. The committee recommended that she should be paired off with somebody of purely British nationality, but was unwilling to dispense with her services altogether for fear of not filling the rota!

The scheme was still in its infancy when, half way through April, the West End had another spectacular raid, possibly the most vicious to date.

The view from our roof was superb and terrifying. This time the show seemed to have been staged for our special benefit, and the enemy gave us everything he had. It was a cold night, with a bitter piercing wind that cut through the thickest clothing and clanged the doors leading from our covered passage to the wide roof garden.

For a time there was only the spitting of distant gunfire as searchlights shot into action, separately sweeping the sky before converging for a moment and then going out. The darkness was followed by comparative silence. Our village lay like a map at our feet.

By leaning over the balustrade of the roof we could peer down into Shepherd Street. There was not a soul to be seen, but a slight chink of light winked at us from Andrey's stationery shop. It went out and a moment later we saw him pass through the door, tighten the scarf round his neck, and walk across the road to join the fire-fighters. The gentlemen's hairdresser's, the grocer's store, the old curiosity shop, the milkman's, the ladies' hairdresser's and the oil store were outlined against a background of more distant streets and houses. A lamp-post glowed to the left, revealing the flattened space where a few weeks ago stood the Shepherd's Cottage, A.D. 1618, and the saddlery. A taxi passed along the street that made the northern borderline of our village, and disappeared in the direction of Park Lane. Suddenly somebody on the fifth or sixth floor of a building a quarter of a mile away lighted a lamp behind a red window blind. The same thing had happened during a recent raid, but behind a green blind. Now was this pure coincidence or a signal? Whatever it was it would take a man at least a quarter of an hour to locate the building, by which time the light would be out.

The drone of a plane could be heard from the south, and gradually the guns began to bark progressively nearer and louder until the big ones quite near us sent their metal screeching into the air. We ran to the wall for cover, knowing that about thirty seconds after these fellows let go we

were apt to receive a rain of shrapnel on the roof. Then to
our right, above the spires and roofs, appeared a cluster of
flares burning with diminishing intensity as they slowly fell
swaying in the wind like a bunch of toy balloons. From the
earth went up to meet them a succession of tracer bullets,
little red balls that seemed to climb terribly slowly to their
quarry. A few flares would be hit and then, deprived of their
parachutes, they would break up and fall swiftly in a score
of dribbling pieces until they seemed to put themselves out
on the housetops.

Aeroplanes soon came over our heads with greater
regularity, and before long one could distinguish the thud
of a bomb, though nothing was seen. The first fires were
not near us. They appeared to burn white first of all. Then
sharp tongues of red flame spat out which painted a scarlet
blob in the sky, deepening at one moment, becoming pale
the next. We watched half a dozen break out and die away
before our own area was involved. At last the bombers
started that exasperating business of turning slowly in
circles which suggests they are looking quietly and methodi-
cally for your own building. Suddenly all the guns in the
area thundered in unison and the noise of the bombs was
drowned. As the tempo quickened bombs began falling
near. We saw them hurling the bricks and mortar of stricken
buildings skywards like waterspouts. Then the air was
filled with minute particles of dust and rubble which, together with the stench of cordite, burned the nostrils.

My companion was a woman at least a head taller than I.
She had the stance of a captain on the bridge of his ship, and
her voice was gruff but warming. One felt that nothing
could happen to a person whose calm assurance made her
discourse on the stars when shrapnel was falling.

From time to time we had visitors. Some of them were
tenants who came up for a friendly chat, and even offered to
relieve us for ten minutes if we felt like a cup of tea; others
whom we did not know by name were doubtless wardens or
from the fire-post below. They looked round with a pro-

fessional air, and occasionally tried to shout to acquaintances on the roof opposite. None of them stayed very long.

After midnight the raid redoubled in fury. A barrage balloon snapped from its moorings, and before it floated past us the cable whipped chimneys and rooftops along its passage with a noise of machine-gun fire. A bomb hurtled through space, and fell with a flash only a short distance away, throwing us on our backs and hurling a piece of pavement up seven storeys to our roof.

How slowly came the hour that preceded the dawn, when the enemy bombers were obliged to go home to their bases! Fires were raging all round us, but it was almost impossible to place them exactly. Was that high corner wall whitened by flames part of the Ritz, or was it in St James's Square or even on the other side of the Thames? The last period of a heavy all-night raid, the period when one knows that it must be over within a quarter of an hour or so, brings a feeling of immense relief. The drone of aeroplanes is less frequent. There are moments when one has nothing else to do but to stare at the magnificently terrifying sight of a city in flames. It is heartbreaking, but spectacular.

Down in the basement the corridor was still crowded when we went there. A multitude of people had come from all the small neighbouring houses to seek protection in our tower of strength. Women wore their best fur coats, eager to save these at least from possible destruction. Their make-up of the evening, like my own, had run with the sweat of fear, and they lay huddled together on the floor. Tommy, our bushy-tailed house-cat, whose nose was severely cut by a piece of flying glass when the garage was bombed, crouched in a corner petrified by the gunfire. I stroked him, and instinctively his back arched and his tail went up.

Our village had suffered hardly any damage. Now that dawn was about to break we wheeled the baby's cot back in the bedroom, and decided to walk across the Green Park to assess the extent of the fires. Piccadilly was slightly scarred. There were broken windows and uprooted gas mains, on which repair gangs were already at work. In the park two policemen were searching for time bombs, one of them carrying an aluminium flare rack dropped by a raider. A wall of flame stretched from Arlington House to the narrow passage by the London Museum. A long line of stately houses, with splendid gardens in which spring flowers were making an untimely appearance, was ablaze. The trees in the park made dancing shadows in the light of the inferno, which was burning itself to extinction. The air was heavy with charred fragments that blew against one's face and clogged one's clothes. We turned past St James's Palace into St James's Street, where we had a presentiment that Christie's was on fire. There was to have been a sale of jewellery, and I had sent a diamond wrist-watch which was being kept with all the other jewels in a safe in the sale-rooms.

As soon as we turned into King Street we knew that our fears were justified. The famous building was burning like a baker's oven—too fiercely for there to be any smoke. The interior was red hot, but in its redness the monumental staircase was clearly outlined. A dozen men were idly watching the scene from the opposite side of the road. Perhaps they were employees who had hoped to save something. When had it happened? How long had it been going on? I had lost too much in the war to worry about a watch, but somewhere in that oven there were £10,000 worth of diamonds and precious stones. How would they come out of this fire? At any rate they would not be covered by insurance.

Bury Street was impassable. What would Quaglino have said if he could have left his Italian village for a few moments to contemplate this part of London he considered his own? The West End was writhing. There was no doubt about that. Its ancient landmarks were passing away. The next generation would not know it as we had. Half Jermyn Street was blocked by mountains of bricks and mortar. I was anxious to walk as far as Long Acre to see if the proofs of a book I had written rather too hurriedly about my flight from the farm in Normandy were ready. The manuscript had already been burned once. It sounds selfish, but one thinks of the strangest things at moments like these. On our way we passed a modern concrete building, the inside of which was burning fiercely. The white façade was now even blackened. On the opposite pavement stood a woman with three small children clinging to her skirts. She was watching the conflagration with tears in her swollen eyes while a sailor was doing his best to comfort her. Was somebody trapped in that building?

The news of the fire at Christie's was published in the newspapers the next morning, and towards the end of the week it was announced that the strong-box with the jewels had been recovered. It was necessary to force it open, and all those who had jewels inside wondered what condition they would be in.

It was fairly obvious that the big diamonds would have suffered no harm at all. My wrist-watch was rather a different matter. In the intense heat the mechanism might have melted.

I was not able to be present at the opening of the safe, which must have presented an interesting study in reactions, but a friend telephoned during the evening to say that everything inside was found to be in perfect condition. Even in these days of shattering events the story caused considerable interest. The sale took place at Derby House, which then stood empty and desolate off Oxford Street on the north side.

Remembered by older generations as Stratford House, this palace of marble, vast windows, and illuminated ceilings was one of the most impressive remaining ghost mansions of another age. The taxi that took me to this sale early one morning in May drove up in a courtyard wide enough for a coach and four to turn with ease. A large printed notice was tied to the monumental staircase advertising the sale by auction of another famous mansion of the Edwardian era. Above the portico of this one also hung a board with the words: 'Freehold for Sale.' It was perhaps no time to cry over the passing of these last remaining mansions. Bricks and mortar had ceased to mean anything.

Climbing to the first floor I passed through a number of lofty rooms, in the last of which a huge coal fire in a white marble fire-place gave a homely touch. There were already fifty or sixty people in the sale-room, most of them seated at a green-baize-covered horseshoe table.

The bowler-hatted jewel experts were watching the slim auctioneer, Mr Terence McKenna, who sported a pink carnation according to custom and to show that nothing could ruffle him. A couple of flickering eyelids fought against each other for an unmounted twelve-carat diamond, the winner carrying it away for £3,500. The battle lasted for less than a hundred seconds.

How quickly had the atmosphere of the famous rooms in King Street been resuscitated! I looked at McKenna, remembering what he had told me a day or two earlier, that three new suits that he had ordered from his tailor were delivered to Christie's on the eve of the fire!

The jewels fetched high prices at this sale, and there was every reason to suppose that the trend would continue upwards. This was the first time within living memory that English people were buying precious stones, valuable pictures, old silver, and even fine furniture simply as a hedge against inflation. Until the war such a state of mind, so prevalent in Europe, was looked on by our people with something akin to contempt.

That evening my husband and I dined at the Apéritif Grill early enough, thanks to double summer-time, to be home before black-out. After leaving the restaurant we walked down Jermyn Street as far as the barrier that cut off the worst raid damage. Pictures had appeared in the papers showing Dunhill's, the pipe-makers, selling their wares on the pavement in front of their devastated premises. Both sides of the street for a distance of a hundred yards had wreckage from which, at about nine o'clock in the evening, several hungry cats would emerge. There was a specially fine white cat that was being made a fuss of that evening by a couple of policemen. They told us that the cats never left the ruins of their former homes during the day, but came out half an hour before dusk. These two fellows with broad shoulders and big hearts saved morsels from their evening meal at the station to prevent the animals from starving. I described the scene in a London paper the next morning, and received letters from generous people all over the country offering to adopt the cats, and even to pay their transportation by train, but the two policemen got into trouble—first for having been together at the barrier, and secondly for feeding cats which, in the eyes of official-dom, have no status. Indeed it was pointed out by the hierarchy of the police world that a motorist does not have to stop after running over a cat, so why should a copper feed one?

Not long after this the sirens sounded for the last but the most ferocious raid of the spring. As soon as it was clear that we were once again the objective, my husband and I wheeled the cot into a corner of the entrance hall between the front door and the living-room. I had a crystal lamp with a shade of pink silk on my table that we put on the floor not to be completely in the dark, and we deadened the light by throwing one of my knitted jumpers over the top.

Never before did so many explosives fall round us. It seemed impossible that our luck would hold out through the night. An hour before midnight the first incendiaries began to fall on our village, and Andrey was only able to save his shop after an hour's frantic work. Soon other little fires were breaking out all over the village. Wardens and fire-fighters clambered on the worn and perilous roofs with stirrup pumps, and our local Phrynes, still with fur coats and high heels, ran hither and thither with pitchers of water.

We might have saved more than we did had not Sunderland House, a massive building nearly half the size of ours, suddenly caught alight. In pre-war days I had known this building with its fine big rooms and crystal chandeliers as a place of charity balls and débutante receptions. It was hired out by the evening. The village people remembered it as the town house of the Duke and Duchess of Marlborough, for whom it had been built by the bride's father, William K. Vanderbilt, as a wedding present. As the fire gathered force a man cried out to me: 'This building is doomed. It was built on consecrated ground—on the site of May Fair chapel!' This philosophical outburst in the face of so much danger staggered me, for it was clear that soon the building would become a raging blaze, and only Andrey's paper shop and a greengrocer's stood between us and the flames. In fact, the entire village might be involved before dawn. While Sunderland House was burning unchecked a young woman, Winifred Berry, who lived in our block of flats, calmly painted the scene from her sitting-room window.

Meanwhile the wardens had broken into a draper's shop to save what they could in the reasonable but erroneous conviction that the place was doomed. Dozens of boxes of silk stockings and newly delivered lingerie were piled under an archway, but as courtesans returned with their pitchers, the boxes disappeared as if by magic. A publican who had put out an incendiary in his restaurant kitchen arrived on the scene with his face covered in soot. He took this incident calmly, remarking that in a previous house that he had managed on the south coast the roof of his establishment had been suddenly wafted away by blast one night like a man's bowler hat in a high wind.

Soon explosives began to fall again, and returning to our entrance hall my husband and I tried to snatch a rest at the foot of the cot. Each time a bomb whistled down we both rose hastily to throw ourselves over the baby as if our bodies could save him from the explosion, but our haste was such that we invariably knocked our heads together on the way up, relieving our fears with laughter.

Incendiaries fell harmlessly in the courtyard, but a terrible stench of burning wool filled the apartment. It was the jumper that I had thrown over the lamp to shield the light. The hot bulb had burned a hole through it.

It was nearly dawn when firemen, worn out with fatigue, arrived to deal with the fires. Soon our main street was oozing with a mixture of water, plaster, soot and broken glass—a horrible pall of smoke and burned wood and paper choked me. The oldest part of the village was still burning, though the firemen, before concentrating on the former ducal mansion, were successful in preventing the flames from spreading. The old houses and shops were left to burn themselves out.

This part of the village was where it communicated with Curzon Street by one of the covered passages between shops and bars. There was a little stone-flagged court on our side of the passage flanked by one-storey houses, with luxuriant gardens on their flat roofs. The whole place had been rather picturesque. There was an open-air flower market in the court, and the tops of the higher houses were crowned with tall, narrow red-brick chimneys and red tiles.

It was not until nearly midday that the shopkeepers whose places had been destroyed began to arrive, for it was Sunday.

Two partners of a little oil shop, of which there was nothing left but a few smouldering sticks, gazed down at the foundations of their once prosperous premises as they might have looked at a freshly dug grave before the coffin of a loved one was lowered into it. They could not be persuaded to leave the place, but poked with their sticks amongst blackened oil drums and twisted metal cases, believing, perhaps, that they would suddenly come upon a treasure.

Their eyes were not always dry, and they turned round and round and walked backwards and forwards on the cobble-stones, only interrupting their miserable thoughts to exchange reminiscences.

Gladys Shearn, who owned the draper's shop, arrived from a western suburb where a time bomb had fallen in the garden of her home during the night. She had lived too long in the village not to be saddened by the disappearance of so many landmarks, but the fire had burned itself out within a few feet of her establishment. This relief was perhaps sufficient to soften the blow of the theft of her silk stockings. The paper shop in the passage (not Andrey's, that still stood safe and sound) had gone entirely, and once it had been hers. She had made her fortune there, and sold it at a big profit.

On the other side of the passage had stood Paillard's, the famous hairdresser's. The place was painted light blue with gold lettering, and I had often paused to examine the superb tortoiseshell hair-combs that were kept in a glass case. They must surely have been relics of Edwardian days. These combs were typical of the artist. Both his manners and his work were of the old school. He had come from France at the beginning of the century to work for the famous Auguste. Auguste took a liking to him, and sent the young man to the beautiful Lady Londonderry of the day. Her ladyship inquired haughtily for Auguste.

'He would not have sent me', came the answer, 'if he had not thought me worthy of the honour.'

For a moment Paillard expected to be sent back to the shop, but Lady Londonderry relented, and he dressed her hair so successfully that she launched him into fame.

On this Sunday afternoon Paillard arrived outside what was left of his shop; an elderly little man, very neat with carefully trimmed moustaches.

'I was intending to hold a slight celebration,' he said with a bitter smile. 'I started here forty years ago this very day. I'm afraid the Nazis have celebrated for me with fireworks.'

Only three days later I received a card from him saying

that he had been given hospitality by a colleague in Knights-bridge, where he was carrying on as usual.

For two days after the great fire in our village our court-yard was filled with soot, charred fragments of bills and cheques and documents of every kind. The wind blew them in eddies, and the flat looked as if all the chimneys had been smoking.

Soon the demolition squads came along, and of the old houses there remained nothing but holes in the ground, the cellars open to the sky. How small these squares looked! It seemed impossible to believe that so many people had lived here, so many flourishing shops done business in so small a space.

Meanwhile the partners of the oil shop became very busy. They rented an empty place adjoining Andrey's paper shop, and having obtained permission from the Government to purchase new stock to the value of what they had lost in the fire, they announced a grand re-opening.

All the village trooped into the house-warming to encour-age these two brave fellows, who beamed with pleasure as they pointed to their shining pots and pans, and exclaimed: 'You know, there's nothing like this left in town!'

But our villagers had also been tempted by the news that the partners had large new stocks of cigarettes, flints, lighters and matches, things which were practically un-obtainable. Towards evening their business became even more brisk. A rumour had gone round that soap was to be rationed. It was not yet true, but the partners sold every bar in the new shop.

Many of our hall porters were being called up, others had left for more profitable work in munition factories. Even 'Hammersmith' had gone. Two women now sat in the entrance hall. They worked the lifts, opened the doors of taxis and motor-cars and carried luggage for men twice as strong as they were.

While waiting for their blue uniforms and gold buttons,

Village vista: Shepherd Market in 1941

Shepherd Market: Ye Grapes

they wore green overalls, and we had nicknamed the younger of the two 'The Goguette', because she was the double of our farmer's wife in Normandy. Each week we gave her our rations of tea that neither of us drank. We tried, whenever possible, to make life a little easier for her. She suffered cruelly from sciatica, and lived in a tiny house near Greenwich, with her old mother and a stepsister of school age.

We did not know all this until one day the Goguette told us that her mother had fallen down the stairs and fractured her thigh. As the little girl was at school the poor woman spent several hours dragging herself to the front door to call a neighbour. She was taken to hospital, where she died.

A few days later the Goguette did not arrive as usual at her work. We thought that she was taking a morning off to wind up her mother's affairs. But she did not come the next day, or the day after that. At the end of the week we heard that she also had died all alone in her humble home. The tenants of the big building in Piccadilly felt suddenly ashamed of themselves for not making inquiries earlier.

CLOTHES rationing was a June baby. It even came as a surprise to the Prime Minister's wife, who said to her milliner while choosing a hat: 'The only inkling my husband gave me was at breakfast when he said in an offhand way: "You ought to buy me some pocket handkerchiefs. They might be rationed one day."'

The milliner smiled with the air of a person who is not affected by bad news, for hats were exempted, and it was too early to foresee the troubles that lay ahead.

People were intrigued rather than angry at the law, for the weather was warm and wardrobes were well stocked. For the few, who by nature felt compelled to get the better of their fellows, there was a loophole in the fact that the trade was given a respite in which to buy materials. Many dressmakers allowed their clients to take advantage of this privilege, and everybody was satisfied. Even when the time limit had lapsed, a little help from here and there worked wonders. One bride who needed a trousseau collected coupons from her mother, her father and four sisters, and doubtless the dressmaker threw in a few of her own to help swell the order. The wedding took place at the country estate of the bride's parents, and as the historic mansion was requisitioned by the military, except for a few rooms at the back where the family still had the right to live, permission was sought from the War Office for the wedding procession to pass through the front entrance.

The most immediate effect of the clothes rationing was not to be found in the big dressmaking houses, or even in the stores, but in the street markets which we had known all our lives.

There was Berwick Market, for instance. But then Soho was changing altogether. Its rather sordid but picturesque streets had been pounded from the air, its shops literally blown into rubble, and half its foreign colony dispersed. It suffered mentally as well as physically. A cosmopolitan, garlic-tainted atmosphere was still to be found there, but misery had gripped it by the throat. The Italians, numerically the strongest and individually the wealthiest, had lorded over Soho at the beginning of the war. They owed their prosperity to the 1914 war when they took the best places in the hotel and restaurant world, and initiated the system of the closed shop. The man-power of the allied nations was otherwise engaged. I am not forgetting the influx of Belgian refugees, some of whom made a little money and opened pastry shops, one of which remained a Soho landmark until it was bombed and moved across the road. But the Belgians took little interest in the hotel world. The Italians wore the most expensive suits, drove the fastest cars and did all the talking. Their hearts swelled with pride during the Abyssinian campaign, and once a week their leaders were invited to Grosvenor Square to drink champagne with Ambassador Grandi in gilt rooms filled with masterpieces from the museums of Florence and Milan.

In September 1939 it looked just possible that history would repeat itself, and that the Italians would continue to make all the money. At any rate that is what they firmly believed. This illusion was shattered when their country entered the war at the time of the French disaster. Those who were not lost in the sinking of the *Arandora Star* were put in concentration camps. Many were later released as friendly aliens, but the spell was broken. Soho's French colony suffered immeasurable hardship. The men, who were mostly cooks, were called up in 1939, and only came back to this country in transit after Dunkirk. They were then sent back to France to continue a war which for them was soon to stop, but by then they were unable to return to their country of adoption, and their families in Soho starved for want of breadwinners.

Berwick Market is through Walker's Court, off Brewer Street, where the pavements used to be encumbered with fruit and vegetable stalls. Walker's Court is narrower than Berwick Street, and forms a bottle-neck. There was a furrier's on one side and a shoe shop on the other. The outside of the furrier's was entirely hidden by all sorts of fur coats hanging out in the open. The shoe shop weathered the storm of clothes rationing, but the furrier's was closed, and the business transferred to another branch. Its façade was boarded up and the door closed with a padlock. This was the first sign that things were going badly.

Berwick Market had a flourishing silk-stocking trade. They were sold from sixpence a pair in barrows, whilst the girls and men from the dress shops that lined the narrow street caught one by the arms and shoulders and tried to hustle one inside. The advent of coupons killed this business, and the silk-stocking barrows disappeared. The famous market now became a peaceful backwater, where an occasional bowler-hatted Hebrew could be seen leaning against a half-empty stall reading a Yiddish newspaper held only a couple of inches from his spectacled eyes. He no longer cried his wares; indeed he gave one the impression of being resigned to a fruitless day. A couple of war policemen, their foreheads hidden by their steel hats, would pass silently and slowly down the middle of the road with an air of complete detachment. An old woman with too much rouge on her wrinkled cheeks and a straw-coloured wig sat on an up-turned basket, gazing at an unimposing stock of men's hose. Seagulls from some Scandinavian fjord, disgusted at the lack of food in Nazi-occupied lands, swooped and pirouetted on a huge A.F.S. lake-sump, from the side of which hung an L.C.C. lifebelt. A small crowd gathered round a cat's-meat stall, and a Negress and a Chinese woman, queerly assorted pair, hurried along arm-in-arm while their shoes clattered noisily on the asphalt.

But in Windmill Street the war had created a new industry. It was to be found half way between London's most famous non-stop variety theatre and the Lex garage. This was the communal lunch.

I came across it shortly before one o'clock on a bright, windy day, when the smoke from the field kitchens in the courtyard blew into my face. This courtyard was the play-ground of St James's and St Peter's school, and housewives looked down upon it from the hundred windows of tall tenement houses as they beat their carpets or hung out their washing.

The smell was appetizing. There was a stew cooking in the big black cauldron. Sacks of potatoes and brussels sprouts lay against the school wall, and already the first customers were filing into the classroom where a smiling woman with tanned features and a flaming red net over her hair sat behind a table at the receipt of custom. There was something incongruous about this daughter of a sunny West Indian isle, transported into the grime of London. She came from Port of Spain, Trinidad, and the L.C.C. restaurant she managed so efficiently was gay and crowded. The walls were covered with travel posters depicting lazy scenes

of the more tropical outposts of the empire; bowls of
flowers splashed vivid colours on the tables, and a radio in
the corner filled the room with the subdued sounds of a
valse. Soho had marked this place with its peculiar stamp.
Guests greeted one another with a nod and a wink, plunged
into animated conversation without hurrying over their
food. The price of the meal was ninepence without a sweet,
and a shilling with plum duff. I took a place in the queue,
handed the money to the lady from Trinidad, and sat down
at one of the long tables.

'Hallo!' said the girl beside me. 'I'm Rhoda, the model.
Do you remember?'

I recalled that she had grown fifty pounds of tomatoes
on a Soho roof at the time we were being told to grow
more food.

'I thought that you and the other girls frequented the
"Blue Mask" in Charlotte Street?' I said.

'It's closed,' she answered.

Then lowering her voice: 'I'm on something good. If
you've got a moment to spare after lunch I'll take you along.'

'Thanks. But tell me, what's happened to the Slade
School?'

In the old days the Slade was in Gower Street, in the
shadow of University College. The students lived in the
old Georgian houses in Fitzroy Street, Charlotte Street and
Fitzroy Square; the models lived close by, where good
rooms could be found for ten shillings a week.

There was a lot of nonsense talked about models. They
worked far too hard to lead a dissipated life. They had to
be punctual for their sittings, and physically strong to stand
the strain. In principle a model earned half a crown an hour,
but she would often pose for a student for two shillings,
and for a friend for a meal. By working hard she could earn
six or seven pounds a week. On Sundays wealthy amateurs
who were working at their normal occupations the rest of
the time were fairly generous. One, for instance, an excellent
painter, was a general at the War Office.

'The Slade?' laughed Rhoda. 'Don't you know that it's been evacuated to Oxford, but most of the students have been called up. Go and have a look round Fitzroy Square. Nearly all the studios have been destroyed during the raids. Those that are left are so shaky that you can hear the walls vibrating as you walk up the stairs.'

'And the models?'

'Many of them are at Oxford, others are in Westmorland, where the Chelsea School of Arts has been evacuated, the rest are in war work. Lydia is a bus conductress on the Putney route, and occasionally punches the tickets of famous painters now in khaki.'

'Are you the only one left?'

'Almost,' said Rhoda. 'There are no more posters to sit for, the shops are not issuing catalogues, and the fashion houses no longer advertise. Even the *Punch* artists are affected by the paper shortage.'

'So that is why the "Blue Mask" is closed. But what has happened to all the little places where one could get a good meal, Italian, German, or French fashion, for one and threepence?'

Rhoda laughed.

'They've closed too. Poor Sally, who painted footsteps on the ceiling of her flat and went to parties with blown hens' eggs in her hair and round her neck, feels that everything is topsy-turvy now. She talks about going back to Australia.'

'What's the story you were going to tell me?'

'You know how difficult it is to get face cream and lipstick? Well, these things are being made in Soho now, and though the face cream smells of paraffin and the lipstick tastes of rancid butter somebody is making a lot of money. There's a factory near here where I drop in when things in the art world are slack. We are paid half a crown an hour, and it's much less tiring than to pose. Would you like to come along and see for yourself?'

'Very well, Rhoda. You lead the way.'

After five minutes' walk we came to a drab street where we stopped in front of a derelict building, which stood between two bombed sites. The upper storeys were obviously uninhabited. The broken windows were covered with grime, and torn blinds fluttered from the casements. The lower part had been a restaurant, and the name of it was still legible. We went down a flight of area steps into a basement, where pink distempered walls, cracked and scarred by blast, were crudely decorated with scenes reminiscent of Harlem. Although the floor was strewn with sawdust, there was a thick undercoating of grease that made it as slippery as ice. Half a dozen men were chopping up chunks of beeswax; others were standing over a line of saucepans on a gas range, and in a corner was a large emulsifying churn controlled by a hand lever.

A good-looking West Indian, wearing a white linen surgeon's overall buttoned up at the back, came across the room to welcome us.

'Charles,' said Rhoda, 'I've brought a girl friend.'

'Fine,' he answered.

Then turning to me, asked: 'Do you know any chemistry? It's my business to draw up the formulae, having been a medical student. Come and take a look at our stock-in-trade: beeswax, liquid paraffin, borax and water. Those four ingredients compose all our products. The machine over here can be geared to several speeds; when the mixture comes out white and viscous, we bottle it as hair fixative; when it's a little less thick, we pot it as face cream, and in the last stage it's excellent as sun-tan or stocking cream.'

Having no qualifications as a chemist, I was relegated with Rhoda to the filling table, where the morning's output of face cream was being put into jars. Our neighbours were a couple of plump housewives, one a Czech, the other a Rumanian; a colleague of Rhoda's who wore a high-necked long-sleeved black frock with three rows of imitation pearls; and lastly two young Jewesses, introduced as Alma and Serena, who both wore corduroy slacks, though one sported royal blue and the other emerald green.

They sang without stopping, the repertoire ranging from Beethoven to the St Louis Blues. A coal-black barber who used to shave all the coloured boxers in London, and who could make good use of strong hair cream to press out the kinks in the woolly mops of his clients, came in with the man who apparently owned this strange factory. I did not ask the owner's name. He was closely shadowed by a body-guard composed of two Italians who were recently in the bottle-party business. This precaution was doubtless neces-sary because of the large sum of money he carried on his person in order to pay for his requirements in cash. A con-signment of metal-capped pots made under Government order to contain anti-gas ointment was transferred to him for £200; another of magenta velvet-covered powder boxes, ordered by a famous Paris firm just before the fall of France, was brought in and stacked against the wall. From his con-versation we gathered that he started life as a planter in British Guiana, and at one period in his career was a member of the Hutterian Brethren, whom he described as a religious sect of farmers who have long beards, wear leather jerkins, sing hymns and till the ground.

On my way home that afternoon I called on Ernest Zaehns-dorf, the bookbinder, whose shop was in the parish of St Giles in the Fields. He was one of the few great craftsmen left in his trade, and his corner showroom, where bookcases filled with superb examples of his handiwork reached nearly to the ceiling, was an ideal place to spend an hour. Ernest Zaehnsdorf's grandfather, Joseph, was born in Budapest a few months after Napoleon had been sent to Elba. He grew up to the sound of the anvil in his father's blacksmith's shop, but as a young man was apprenticed to a bookbinder at Stuttgart.

After a few years he came to London, started a business of his own, and soon became famous. His son carried on after him, having widened his knowledge in Paris, where he was trapped during the siege while staying with his uncle, court jeweller to Napoleon III.

Ernest Zaehnsdorf was thus a craftsman with the inherited cunning of three generations. There may be no more like him, for the old system of apprenticeship was finished, and young men found easier ways of making money. For the lover of books this was a tragedy.

Zaehnsdorf's building had suffered considerably from blast during the air raids. The windows had no longer any glass, and it had been replaced by a semi-transparent material. The workmen carried on with great devotion, and for this future generations would have reason to be grateful.

One cold January morning Mr Zaehnsdorf's telephone rang, and the librarian of the stricken Guildhall announced that two thousand priceless volumes had been saved from the fire, but were soaked by the firemen's hoses. There were reference books on London that existed in no other library, and copies of the *London Gazette* dating back one hundred and fifty years. A van was sent round to collect these precious volumes, which were then opened out on benches, on tables, on chairs, and all over the floors, where they were subjected to gentle heat from coke fires for nearly two months. From time to time, if there were any signs of the leaves of a book warping, these were placed for twenty-four hours in a press, and then laid out to dry again.

These were the light casualties.

Some books were partly burned, others were torn to ribbons. These urgent cases did not come only from the Guildhall, but from all over London. The vellum charter of London University, three sheets with a seal at the bottom, had been flayed by chunks of cement hurled by the explosion through the steel walls of the deed-box in which it was kept, and then churned round inside. Just as a surgeon puts new skin on an injured face, experts grafted new vellum on the torn charter, and carefully drew on it a facsimile of the original text.

One book from the university was found to have a small sea-shell embedded in a hole an inch deep. How had this fragile shell been hurled through the boards of the binding to land unbroken inside? Possibly the shell had been released from a wall when the cement was pulverized by the explosion. But then it must have been a piece of cement that opened up the way for the shell into the heart of the book. This was only one of the great unexplained mysteries of high explosives.

From London University also came many volumes of the famous De Morgan collection of very early mathematical books of the sixteenth and seventeenth centuries, blasted and cut, and with their backs slashed; a first edition of Johnson's *Dictionary* in two volumes (1755); and one of Gerard's *Herball* (1597), into which the dust was forced with such velocity that it had to be removed from the pages with special rubber that dry-cleans without harming the surface.

The charter and by-laws of the Loriners' Company were in a strong-room in the cellars of Carpenters' Hall (Throgmorton Avenue) when that building was destroyed by fire. Owing to the dangerous condition of the walls it was not until six months after the fire that anybody was allowed to search the ruins and remove the contents of the safe. By this time the historic documents were soaked and covered with mildew. This called for the most delicate of operations.

After the sheets of vellum were dried they were sprayed with a mixture of paradichlor and orthodichlor benzine in solution from an ordinary garden spray, which entirely killed the mildew. The seals in this case withstood the damp.

This was by no means the worst of such cases. Sir Banister Fletcher's original drawings for his *History of Architecture* were dripping wet, with the sheets stuck fast together, when they were finally retrieved from the Chancery Lane Safe

Deposit, three months after the dreadful fire that destroyed half the famous street. The drawings in a thoroughly sodden state smelt so appallingly bad that the workmen were tempted to use their gas masks while handling them. The drawings were repaired with such cunning, however, that future generations will never realize how near they were to destruction.

Mr Zaehnsdorf was generally to be found in his little office behind the showroom. It was a dark but homely hide-out, with an anthracite stove fitted with one of those little windows through which one can see the red coals. A couple of kettles on the boil invariably stood on top of the stove; above this a clock ticked away in a niche surrounded by files and reference works that had been collected for over half a century.

'What would you say if I asked you to bind a book for me?' I queried.

'We would do our best,' answered Mr Zaehnsdorf, 'but things are becoming very difficult. Take gold-leaf, for instance. The ancients discovered that nothing else would do for tooling and lettering a book. Indeed it was used by the Egyptians for decorative purposes. Everything but gold-leaf tarnishes, but now I see that even jewellers will not be allowed to make wedding rings of more than nine-carat gold, and when I went to my gold-beater this morning he warned me that we might soon have no more gold-leaf.

'And the leather? If you intend to bind a book I suggest that you choose a skin, for we shall have to wait at least six months for another lot. The millboard is also practically impossible to obtain, while next month one of my most expert workmen is to be called up.'

The office where we sat looked out on Earlham Street.

There used to be a flourishing street market here, for it leads straight into Seven Dials, through which Ernest Zaehnsdorf's father walked in the eighties gripping a stout stick when he returned at night to his home in York Street, Strand.

Those were the days when the police patrolled Seven Dials in pairs because of the footpads. Ernest kept the stick his father used for this journey and showed it on occasion with pride.

The war brought the crow of the cock and the cackle of the goose to Seven Dials; there was, in fact, a complete farmyard in the heart of W.C.1, for which the entire neighbourhood became famous.

The farm was a family venture that started when Private O'Doherty of the Irish Guards bought twenty-four Rhode Island Reds a week old for three shillings apiece, and installed them in King's Head Yard, which retains all the picturesqueness of its three centuries of unchanged existence.

The King's Head was a costermonger's yard, and belonged to Private O'Doherty's father, a little man with a birdlike, spectacled face, whose business it was to make and mend coster barrows.

Mr O'Doherty plied his age-old trade in a workshop which belonged to his sister-in-law, Nelly Keeley. It was on the other side of the road. The place was really a marketman's warehouse of the type so common at Covent Garden: that which is closed by a roll-down iron shutter embracing the whole façade. Instead of the sacks of potatoes and cases of apples which one sees in the fruit and vegetable market, there was simply a handbarrow at the entrance with a notice hung over one of the handles stating the cost of its weekly rental. Inside were coster barrows in varying stages of completion, and at the back a carpenter's bench well fitted with tools. The place must have been old, because O'Doherty stated that he could be sure of all its history since a certain Peter Murray of Nottingham Court was installed there in 1833. Peter Murray sold the business to Tom Colman, who eventually disposed of it to the Keeleys, then fishmongers in Peter Street, Soho.

The Keeleys had made a position for themselves by honesty and hard work. Nellie Keeley was seventy-six, and head of the firm. Her chief interests were in the flower business, and she had a shop which was also her home in Short's Gardens, where she and her two younger sisters made wreaths and wedding bouquets.

In the days of Peter Murray, at least a century ago, barrows were let out to costers at threepence a day, since when, curiously enough, there was practically no increase. At one period just before the war, when costers could make up to three pounds a day by selling fruit in busy streets, Mr O'Doherty had raised the price to fourpence, but he soon discovered that competitors were giving a penny back.

Until fruit became almost unobtainable O'Doherty had two hundred barrows always on hire. Then the business slumped. Young costers were called up for military service, and there was hardly anything in the market to sell. Nevertheless Mr O'Doherty took a pride in keeping his barrows in good repair, although he was only allowed twenty shillings' worth of timber a month, which he took in ash.

Some of the barrows were kept in King's Head Yard with the Rhode Island Reds, and all the other animals and birds in the farmyard. There were also seventeen ducks and drakes, a goat in kid, some geese, two she-cats with kittens, and the pony that Mr O'Doherty's neighbour kept there to draw his cart. The hens laid well at a time when eggs were rationed at two a month for each person. The ducks laid well also, but anywhere they took a fancy to in the borough, and they were careful to hide their eggs so that nobody could find them. They also discovered the local A.F.S. deep-water sump, into which they waddled to the delight of passers-by.

The youngest of the Keeley sisters (Mr O'Doherty had married the second) took the money from the costers at the end of their day. Most of the barrows were stored in another yard, where there was a dilapidated shed in which cows were kept in Peter Murray's day.

When there was a wedding order the three sisters used to meet in the flower shop in Short's Gardens and make up the bouquets round the big table in the centre of the warm, cosy room, while the canaries and the love-birds sang in their cages, and the radio played a tune. This sitting-room was a Victorian period piece, with a fine picture of Nellie in her young days, when waists were slim and hair done up in a bun behind the head. There had been a show window to display the flowers, but this was blown out by a bomb, and the front was now boarded up but, as Mrs O'Doherty remarked, it didn't matter much because most of their work was to order, and there were no longer any passers-by along Short's Gardens.

The three sisters, and the canaries and the love-birds sheltered in the basement kitchen during all the air raids, but now life was normal again, and they were enjoying the quiet evenings. A bright coal fire burned merrily in the hearth, casting a rosy glow over the gaudy flowered wall-paper, and the big ornamental oak sideboard on which were neatly ranged the family photographs and heirlooms. 'It is our house now,' they explained. 'We have worked for it and are proud of it.' And they kept it spick and span, and wore green overalls when making the bouquets that young Miss O'Doherty delivered in the van when she was back from the ambulance station where she worked as her contribution to the war effort. Her mother spoke of her driving with tears of admiration. 'She can see in the dark,' said Mrs O'Doherty. 'Real cat's eyes. And the way she turns a car! It's wonderful.'

A SANDWICH man disguised as a Father Christmas leaned wearily against the rusted cigarette machine of a tobacconist's shop in Piccadilly Circus, his board pointing a wooden finger at an adjoining newsreel cinema. This individual with his shabby scarlet cloak and not very white beard was the only outward sign that the heart of the empire was about to celebrate the third Christmas of the war. The shops did not give the impression of being loaded with a superfluity of goods. Silk stockings had disappeared by now. When, on rare occasions, stocks were released by the Government, the fact was advertised in the newspapers, and each consignment of several thousand pairs sold within a few hours to women who had started to queue up when it was still dark in the morning.

Turkeys and geese did not hang in barbaric profusion outside the poulterers' in Soho. Only clients who had ordered birds at least a month in advance were certain of having them. Coty, in Bond Street, opened for one and a half hours in the morning, and for the same time in the afternoon, and before each opening long queues formed outside. Women were fortunate to obtain a box of face powder or a lipstick. Charbonnel and Walker had few chocolates to sell to passers-by. Their small stocks were bespoken.

In spite of these things there was a great effervescence in the streets. London had not been so full since the war began, and anybody who arrived from the provinces was obliged to try at least a dozen hotels before finding a vacant room. The Savoy, in order to disappoint as few people as possible, turned part of its famous underground air-raid shelter into a dormitory, and people were glad to take advantage of this arrangement. The restaurants were filled to capacity, and people were not unwilling to pay three pounds for a bottle of champagne and half a guinea for a drop of gin. The desire to spend money was staggering. Business was only limited to the stocks in hand. Oxford Street, Regent Street and Piccadilly were crowded until the official closing hour for shops at 4 p.m., and people took home their gifts without the traditional paper wrapping. London had once again become the great metropolis with its jostling crowds. During the raids it was the city of the brave and the few. Now thousands of children had come back from the reception areas, and even the most cautious of grown-ups felt they could risk a few nights in town. Every flat in our great block was occupied, and the motor cars drove in and out of the courtyard until the small hours of the morning, filling the night air with the gases from their exhaust pipes, the drivers ignorant or uncaring of the risks our sailors took to bring the precious petrol across the sea.

The cocktail bars in Piccadilly were crowded with soldiers, sailors and airmen, not only of the home country, but of the Dominions and the free allied nations. Norwegians and Dutch, French and Poles in their respective uniforms crowded the hotel foyers. Some airmen and a few technicians back from Murmansk and Leningrad told stories of the Russian campaign fought in temperatures of twenty to thirty degrees below zero. A young officer wearing picturesque headgear with the wide brim turned up on one side and decorated with a bunch of bright green feathers was just back from Gambia, where the temperature on the day of his departure registered one hundred in the shade.

Covent Garden, in spite of all its difficulties, had a busy morning on the day before Christmas. There were fir trees in plenty, a good deal of holly and a fair supply of mistletoe. Most of the dealings in vegetables were confined to sacks of potatoes, carrots and cauliflowers, and there was a little rhubarb, though it was expensive.

The central aisle, where in peace time Poupart and Solomon displayed luxury fruit from every part of the world, had some difficulty in making a show. Their windows were filled with pears, red Canadian apples and a few black grapes, augmented with bottles of ginger wine cordial. A few market men came back on leave in sailors' uniform to exchange greetings with their pals still at work. The big bomb crater next to Solomon's was still an unsightly cavern, half filled with rubble, broken umbrellas, smashed market baskets and pulverized brick. The owner of a famous restaurant told me that he was just off to buy half a dozen bottles of Grand Marnier at five pounds each, which he considered a bargain. A year earlier the price was considered high at twenty-five shillings.

While I was giving a bath to my child, the door-bell rang and an elderly man who lived in our block of flats came to wish me a happy Christmas.

'It is not a happy one for me,' he said sadly. 'My wife was caught in our villa at Monaco when France fell. Neither she nor I are young, and sometimes I wonder if we shall ever see one another again.'

There was an utter weariness in his voice. He had been wandering through the streets all day, shocked by the apparent heedlessness of the crowds to the mental anguish of others.

There could be no enjoyment out of turkey and Christmas pudding for this lover of seventy-odd years who pictured his wife starving in the mocking sunshine of the Riviera.

I soon realized that he had come for feminine sympathy. He wanted in his agonizing unhappiness to find a woman capable of understanding what it meant for him to be so utterly alone, and the fact that we had hardly met before was not of the slightest importance.

He took the last letter he had received from his wife out of an inside pocket, and read me a few passages in which she described how all the members of the British colony had been obliged to attend local courts where they were asked searching questions to discover any Jewish blood. British citizens were not allowed to leave Monaco, and those who were still there considered themselves lucky, for many had been sent to concentration camps inland. Milk and meat were unobtainable, but the Hôtel de Paris at Monte Carlo occasionally put rabbit on its menu, though only residents and their guests were served. She had just had her wireless set taken away, and was thus finally deprived of the satisfaction of hearing any news of England.

I asked if he had tried to bring her home, but he answered that he had never tried to influence her one way or another, in which he was probably right. Many who were successful in reaching Lisbon lost their lives when ships were torpedoed and dive-bombed, and it was impossible to obtain a seat on a homeward-bound air liner.

He folded his letter and put it carefully back into his pocket, whereupon he rose to go. I could see that he felt better now, and I made no effort to prevent him from leaving.

Our village was practically deserted over the holidays, and many of the shopkeepers decided not to reopen until Monday, which gave them four whole days at home. Their absence was reflected in a more generous milk distribution, which before Christmas was very short. The weather turned suddenly cold, and on Sunday, for the first time, thin ice could be seen on some of the lake-sumps.

I decided to attend matins at St James's, Piccadilly. Only the south aisle remained standing after high explosives and incendiaries had rained on both the church and the adjoining rectory during the night raids of the summer.

St James's was the essence of Piccadilly. Wrecked and charred, it continued to arrest the attention of the passer-by as the most spectacular ruin of the neighbourhood.

My first interest in St James's was when, as a very young woman, it was pointed out to me that the steeple was sloping. This had struck me so deeply that I never once walked past without looking up at it with fascination. This steeple was the only part of the church for which Wren was not responsible; his original design was refused on the ground of expense, and the work was given to a local builder.

What gave the church its picturesqueness was the open-air pulpit, the big yard paved with old tombstones which originally stood upright, and the gnarled tree which in summer spread its leafy branches almost over Piccadilly.

This courtyard was now filled with all the debris of the bombed church and rectory, and at the foot of the tree in its

winter nakedness stood a heap of twisted metal and a notice
to the effect that the emergency work was being done by
X & Co. A low wood fence was erected against Piccadilly,
and in the place of Sir Reginald Blomfield's fine modern
entrance gates of wrought iron was a notice in red, yellow
and green lettering, giving the hours of the services. The
rectory where the aged verger and his wife were killed was
razed to the ground; of the open-air pulpit only the canopy
remained. A damp musty smell met one in the church. In
an ante-room were piled thirty or forty gravestones, an
electric fuse-box on which one could still read, 'Danger—
400 volts', the remains of a kitchen range, the coat of arms
of William and Mary, with a piece of green baize thrown
over the heads of the lion and unicorn, and a broken kitchen
chair.

What struck one most here was a great chest with iron
bands, two huge padlocks, and immense rings. Some people
said it came from the Spanish Armada, others believed it to
be of Germanic origin.

In another ante-room below the belfry was the great bell
that crashed to the ground during the fire. A piece of rope
by which it was tolled was still visible hanging from the
ceiling. One plaque remained untouched by fire. It read:

'Near this place are deposited the remains of William Van
de Velde, the elder, who died in 1693; and of his son who
died in 1707. After the year 1673 these eminent Dutch
marine artists lived and worked in this country as painters
of sea fights for Their Majesties King Charles the Second
and King James the Second.'

If one removed two empty oil cans from the door and
neglected the warning, 'Danger—Keep out', it was possible
to enter the church itself and look through the charred
timber of what had once been the roof at the sky above.

All was utter desolation, smelling of fire, water, and decay.
The pews were piled in the north aisle, and on the ground
the soil of the earth had been turned up. There were fragments of an old piano, pieces of wood and metal.

But the south aisle was bricked up. This was the only part of the church where a service could be held, and when I passed in I found a dozen people kneeling, for the service had already begun.

A strip of blue and silver lamé covered the scarred wall behind the altar, and holly and chrysanthemums were in profusion. The windows were covered with a semi-transparent material which flapped with the north wind, but which allowed the late December sun to penetrate and light up the cross with its golden rays.

The whitewash on the walls had peeled because of the damp, and the ceiling was covered with some substance that looked strangely like brown paper. The offertory box by the door bore the notice: 'We have lost much—Please give generously.'

A woman sat in front of a piano to the right of the altar, playing the music for the hymns and the responses. She replaced with this piano the seventeenth-century organ with its gilded angels carved by Grinling Gibbons, which had once graced the church (and which was fortunately saved from destruction). The boys in the choir wore frills and the girls had sky-blue veils. It was bitterly cold, and the traffic in Jermyn Street roared past, with nothing but the flimsy material in the windows to deaden the noise.

But in spite of all this, or perhaps because of it, no service has ever seemed so real to me. The cloth backs of the prayer-books were warped with long immersion, and the pages stained and singed. One felt honoured to use them.

Men with special goggles to protect their eyes had, for some time, been removing the big iron railings round the parks. They used flame cutters, that threw up a curtain of glittering sparks against the grey winter background.

As I turned into Piccadilly from Down Street on the morning of New Year's Eve I gave a little gasp of surprise at the depth of the landscape facing me. Now that the tall railings had gone Piccadilly looked as if it was transported by magic into the heart of the country. An orange sun was trying to pierce the haze that hid Buckingham Palace from view, and it looked for all the world as if the green grass with its coating of frost and the gaunt naked trees must stretch away into the infinite. Two gardeners, leaning against their rakes, were watching a great bonfire that sent smoke curling into the distance, and a thick carpet of curled-up brown leaves, smelling of damp moss, overflowed on the pavement that was now one with the park.

For the first time the beauty of London was being revealed. Everywhere the eye was charmed by vistas that none of us had quite suspected. Our squares seemed larger and more noble, and Park Lane grew into a broader avenue where one breathed more easily the good air of the country. Even the gardens bordering Hamilton Place, which the royal princesses played when the king and queen lived in Piccadilly, had shaken off their iron bands, allowing shrubs and trees to stretch black, sooty branches across the pavement.

I had promised to meet a friend in Leicester Square which now most miserably bore witness not only to the damage to Poulsen's Café de Paris but to much larger devastation on all sides from a number of vicious fire raids, so that the famous song of the 1914 war had acquired an ironical undertone.

In pre-war days I am not sure that Leicester Square did not need to be seen at night. Its lights were, on the whole, more brilliant than those in the Circus, and its interests—cinemas, theatres, night clubs and bottle parties—were mostly nocturnal.

But, I thought, if ever I lived to see it lighted again not a myriad of electric bulbs would be able to dim the picture I carried with me of the great fires that had earlier raged between the Odeon and the Warner cinemas, singeing the ghosts of the Alhambra and Daly's. The whole square was then a sea of broken glass, and flames painted it in scarlet under a blue-black sky in which throbbed the drone of distant planes. The Café Anglais had escaped the big fire by a miracle. The flames had licked it but had respected the ornamental garden façade where shrubs in pots stood between green pillars. Beside it, built on the ruins of the fire, was a huge lake-sump, large enough to attract the seagulls.

Shakespeare, with his chin resting on his right fist, gazed morosely and probably with a tinge of jealousy at the queue for *Gone with the Wind*, the biggest box-office success of the decade. The bard had lost his left hand in one of the night raids, and his garden was mutilated with air-raid trenches that nobody had yet used. The iron railings had been taken from the square for salvage, and had been replaced by wicker stakes. But at the poet's feet, some thoughtful gardener had planted three rows of wallflowers which would add a touch of colour in the early summer.

I had no personal desire to celebrate New Year's Eve, but towards 10 p.m. some friends prevailed on me to make a quick tour with them round the Piccadilly night spots to see what was going on. We arrived at the first smart hotel to find the arc lights turned on the cabaret—a couple singing rather coarse, lurid songs greeted with heavy laughter. There were some splendid uniforms, and quite a lot of tail suits and white ties, which seemed as strange and out of place as uniforms would have done three years before. A little man in a neat brown suit brushed past me as I stood in the passage, muttering between his teeth: 'All those people should be wearing black arm-bands to mourn the loss of Hong Kong instead of playing the fool. . . .' He sped towards the street swing-doors, colliding with a young Polish officer who called to the night porter:

'Can we dance in here?'

'No room, sir. It's absolutely full.'

'No room to dance on New Year's Eve?' echoed the officer, disgusted, as he swung himself out into the night again.

In Regent Street the monster cafés were filled with picturesque crowds. At one of them where there is a space between the darkness of the night and the brilliant lights of the bar—a sort of dim, curtained-off ante-room—a subaltern was fast asleep on a worn canopy snoring away his drunkenness, legs stretched out at their full length on the floor. In the foyer two young girls, waiting for their male companions who had gone to fetch their coats, talked in shrill voices, their cheeks flushed with wine. Said one of them: 'How can one get sentimental with a man who talks about nothing but aeroplane engines?'

Officers with paper hats picked their way gingerly down the stairs carrying glasses. The head waiter of the grill slammed the glass doors of his domain in the faces of queueing guests, shouting: 'It's full up now.' Somebody started to hum *Tipperary*.

1942

1942

OUR village was built on the spot, then all green fields with wild bugloss bushes, where Edward I privileged the hospital of St James to keep an annual fair 'on the eve of St James, the day and the morrow, and four days following'.

These fields, through which the Tybourne stream 'wound between banks and braes, fringed with rushes and redolent with wild mint',[1] were known as Brook Fields, and as time went on the fair was called May Fair. The first three days were for serious trading in cattle and leather, while the rest of the time was for amusement.

'The Cottage, A.D. 1618', which by a miracle remained in perfect condition until German night raiders blew it up in 1940, was originally the home of a herdsman who looked after the cattle during the annual fair. With the destruction of this tiny cottage we lost our oldest link with the past.

By the year 1701 the popularity of the fair was so great that its attractions were increased. The ground floor of the Market House, usually occupied by butchers' stalls, was appropriated, during the fair, to the sale of toys and gingerbread, and the upper portion was converted into a theatre. The open space westward was covered with the booths of jugglers, fencers and boxers, with the stands of mountebanks and swings and roundabouts. The sides of the street were filled with sausage stalls and gambling tables. The first-floor windows served as the proscenia of puppet-shows.

Whereas the shepherd of 'The Cottage' had lived in the depths of the country, London in 1701 was now creeping

[1] *Mary Davies and the Manor of Eburys*, by Charles Gatty.

towards the May Fair. St James's Church had been finished in 1684, and its churchyard faced Piccadilly Street, alias Portugal Street.

Londoners were only just beginning to talk about Piccadilly. It was the name of a very short stretch of road running no farther west than Sackville Street. From here to Stratton Street the thoroughfare was called Portugal Street in honour of Charles the Second's wife, and all beyond was the 'way to Reding' or 'Hide Park Road', along which coaches frequently overturned or were stopped by highwaymen. The Tybourne stream passed into Green Park under a stone bridge at the top of what is now Brick Street. It still flows, but underground, in an arched culvert under Clarges Street and Curzon Street, and for a short distance along Half Moon Street, then across Whitehorse Street to Brick Street on its way to the Thames.

There was a turnpike at the end of Berkeley Street and the town did not extend farther than Berkeley House, which later gave place to Devonshire House.

To the north of our village in 1708 was a low house with a garden embowered in a grove of plane trees. Here lived Mr Edward Shepherd. You will locate his mansion better if I tell you that it eventually became Crewe House in Curzon Street.

In this year (1708) Mr Shepherd had seen a lot of disorderly behaviour at the May Fair, so much that the fair was abolished by a Grand Jury presentment: '. . . the yearly riotous and tumultuous assembly in a place called Brook Field, in the Parish of St Martin-in-the-Fields, called May Fair. In which place many loose, idle, and disorderly persons did rendezvous, draw, and allure young persons, servants, and others to meet there to game and commit lewdness.'

Was this to be the end of May Fair, which had existed through so many centuries? It appeared so for the moment, but very soon Londoners returned to their evil ways. The place was too ideally situated, and in Carrington Street there was the Dog and Duck Tavern behind which was a pond two hundred feet square, where the sport of duck hunting was beloved not only by the butchers, but also by the people of quality. The fair came back, but gradually part of the ground was built over. Mr Shepherd noticed that the market value of the land made building operations more remunerative than cattle dealing. A church called May Fair Chapel, or Curzon Chapel, was put up in 1730, opposite Mr Shepherd's own mansion. Its incumbent, the Rev. Alexander Keith, later made a fortune by marrying people without banns or licence in a house close by called Keith's Chapel, which became more notorious even than Gretna Green for runaway marriages—an aristocratic rival of the Fleet Prison for irregular unions. May Fair Chapel was eventually bought by Vanderbilt, who pulled it down to build a mansion for his daughter, Consuelo, when she married the Duke of Marlborough. He was warned that to build on consecrated ground would not only make the marriage unhappy, but would also cause his daughter's home to perish by fire. The marriage was a failure. The mansion, known as Sunderland House, was gutted in the great air raid in May, when so much of our market was burned.

Shortly after May Fair Chapel was built streets were planned. Already there was Clarges Street, and then came Half Moon Street, named after an inn. Mr Shepherd, watching London spread westward, bought the irregular open space on which May Fair had been held since the days of Edward I and, in 1735, built Shepherd Market. The butchers' shops had theatres on the second stories, where plays were given during the fair. A passage called Whitehorse Street was made to connect the market with what, by then, was known to everybody as Piccadilly.

Nowadays Whitehorse Street is not wide enough for two cars to pass unless one of them mounts the pavement. Along it are the area basements of club kitchens. The walls are dark and windowless. I passed along it one foggy January morning to lunch with Colonel Tempest Stone, secretary of the Naval and Military. This club is known to

Londoners as the 'In and Out', because of the bold signs in Piccadilly directing traffic into the courtyard by one gate and out by the other.

The house was built in 1760, a time when the mean buildings on the north side of Piccadilly were being pulled down to make way for the mansions of wealthy people. The second Earl of Egremont owned it, and after his death his son, who won the Derby and the Oaks each five times, and the Gold Cup at Goodwood in the first year of its institution, spent some years there. London was then becoming modernized. Short-stage coaches conveyed passengers to every village round the town for sixpence or a shilling. At every street corner porters stood to carry parcels or run errands. They were licensed, and wore a badge. The shops kept open till eight or nine, and their lights made the streets agreeable. In addition to the usual oil lamps, as many as twenty candles were placed in the shop windows, giving a delightful effect.

In due course Egremont House became Cambridge House, and there Queen Victoria was attacked by a madman as she stepped into her carriage to drive away across the cobbled courtyard. Later it became Palmerston House. When Lord Palmerston died his body was brought there before being taken to Westminster Abbey.

Egremont, Cambridge, Palmerston. . . . We then come to the quiet, luxurious sixties, when a party of officers, mostly from The Buffs quartered at the Tower of London, decided to start a club of their own because all those that catered for the services were full. They called it the Naval and Military.

The club-house was struck by one out of a stick of five bombs that straddled Piccadilly from the Green Park to Whitehorse Street. It hit the drawing-room at a slant, and sent the room with the furniture crashing down into the hall where the porter and the telephone girl emerged safe but covered with dust and debris. It also entirely wrecked the ladies' drawing-room on the second floor, as well as several card rooms and thirty-one out of forty-four bedrooms.

The Naval and Military provided facilities for entertaining women guests in 1919, but was by no means the first service club to do so, the Junior Naval and Military having made similar arrangements in the late nineties. But the senior club went a step further in 1934 by allowing women relations to become associate members with their own quarters.

The bomb was more unkind to the women than to the men, for it almost obliterated their living space, but when the club was cleaned up the men came gallantly to the rescue, sharing the accommodation left to them. Thus the coffee room was divided by a curtain, and the regimental dining-room became a salon for feminine chatter.

Our village had a modern Mr Shepherd. His name was George William Hayward, and he was eighty-seven.

George Hayward began life as a farmer's boy in Essex. In 1869, at the age of fourteen, he slung a bundle over his shoulder and walked to London in search of adventure. Attracted by the wide sweep of Piccadilly he resolved to work in the heart of the West End and knocked at the door of a private house in Half Moon Street, where the butler set him cleaning the boots and polishing the silver.

The germ of success was in Hayward's blood. He worked longer hours than the other boys in the street, and his boots and silver shone brighter. When the aged butler died, the wealthy owner of this house had come to consider the boy so indispensable that he raised his wages and took no other servant. George learned to cook and to press clothes and brush the silk of a top-hat. In the evening he attended night school, where the farm-boy learned French and German so that when his employer travelled to a German spa or to a French watering-place George accompanied him as a courier, looking after his tickets, buying his food in the markets, and cooking it the way English people liked it.

Sometimes good servants are rewarded for their labours. This happened in the case of George Hayward. He was left £100 in the old gentleman's will, and, anxious with this money to develop his business instincts, he took a walk into Shepherd Market, where he found a small shop at a modest rental. Within a few months he had opened a grocer's store, but as nearly all his capital had gone in paying the first quarter in advance, and purchasing the furniture and stock, he could only buy new goods with the takings of the previous day. Wholesalers were suspicious of him. They refused to grant him credit, so, from time to time, George went to Harrods, where he bought his groceries retail, like any ordinary customer, hoping to resell them at a profit to the large houses in his neighbourhood. Mr Harrod got to hear of this and, impressed by the young man's enthusiasm, gave him the credit that the wholesalers had refused and charged him a little less than retail prices.

George worked fourteen hours a day single-handed. Then he married, and his wife helped in the store.

Soon the place became too small, and George moved across the road to a larger shop, and when this also became too small he rented an adjoining one and knocked the two together. His store was now quite famous. It was the largest establishment in the village. Butlers and liveried footmen came there from all the big mansions in Curzon Street and Hertford Street, in Half Moon Street and Clarges Street. His clients were the ladies and gentlemen of the nobility. They bought the very best, and though they were not always very prompt in paying, the accounts were never questioned.

One day a candle and oil shop at the corner of the marketplace went bankrupt. George looked into his bank account and saw that he had enough to take it over and nurse it for a year. Long before that the corner shop started to make money. The same thing happened when he took over the greengrocer's. When the butcher's shop got into financial straits, George was fired with the memory of Mr Shepherd, whose butcher's shop had theatres on the second storeys. He felt that it was the heritage of the market to deal in beef and mutton, and as he now had three young sons he bought the butcher's shop, and put in one of his sons as manager.

Observe that there was none of the big-store complex about George.

Nobody coming into the market for the first time would be aware of these wide interests of George Hayward. The village still had its little shops, and they were undoubtedly old-fashioned and picturesque, grouped with individuality like clumps of flowers in a garden. Each of them, of course, was called Hayward. In fact, if the grocer ran out of candles, he would direct you with the greatest courtesy to the oil shop up the street, and people who did not know went away from the village wondering at this politeness of a past age.

George then acquired the pork shop opposite the covered passage leading into the market from Curzon Street. He wanted his clients to have their sausages according to their tastes. This noble earl or that liked a little more pepper or a little less spice. Butlers now reported a demand for china with the ancestral crest. This was too much for the oil shop. George decided to open a china shop opposite to deal with the coronets and monograms.

This all happened before the First World War. Alas, things had changed when we lived there, and there were fewer wealthy lords, fewer large houses and no butlers or footmen. George was too old to look after his shops, and though he was still the village headman he lived in a quiet spot on the east coast overlooking the North Sea. His son William, who once played truant and ran away to Canada, had his father's dim little office above the grocer's shop. A narrow, creaking staircase led to his sanctum, from behind the cash desk where his wife was generally to be found. William sat at a desk littered with bills and invoices, and stacked with tins of pineapple and condensed milk. There was nothing of the big business man about him. His voice was quiet and unassuming, almost plaintive. From time to time he would come down to lend a hand in the shop or to pass hurriedly along the village main street in his long white coat on the way to the greengrocery or the pork butcher's or the oil shop.

'How's business, Mr Hayward?'

'There's plenty of business within limitations. But consider the shortage of staff, and the controlled prices, and the rationing, and the hundreds of forms I have to fill in every day. Yes, business is good these days when we don't lose too much money.'

It is the privilege of the London tradesman to grumble cheerfully.

'I don't doubt that you have a few pennies put aside for a rainy day,' I said, smiling.

William Hayward pointed to the brick-bound foundations of what, before the great fire, had been flourishing little eighteenth-century buildings. There was nothing left of them but small geometrical squares half filled with water and rubble.

'My father never lost a farmer's instinct for putting his savings into property,' he said. 'Those wretched-looking rubbish heaps that I could jump right over if I took a bit of a run cost him over £10,000. Now, madam, I leave you to figure out what they'll be worth after the war.'

THE Americans came to our village in the chilly fogs of March. They wore battle dress and forage caps, and hailed from anywhere and everywhere between Oregon and Maine and North Dakota and Texas. After dark they moved like shadows along Piccadilly, straining their eyes, unaccustomed to the black-out, for a feminine silhouette to engage in conversation. They brought into our anxious lives a sudden exhilaration, the exciting feeling that we were still young and attractive and that it was tremendous fun for a young woman to be courted, however harmlessly, by quantities of generous, eager, film-star-ish young men who spoke and behaved in an appealingly different manner from that to which she was accustomed. Their presence everywhere stimulated parties, made excuses for people to get together, and they introduced new topics of conversation, an awareness that life was not after all only tears and suffering. I felt myself, in common with the entire feminine population, vibrating to a new current in the spring air, anxious to please, determined to recover if only temporarily some small taste of pre-war glamour. Soon the streets became full of these young men who stood in groups at the top of Whitehorse Street, humming tunes we Londoners did not recognize, whistling admiringly when I passed with the pram and the pekinese, offering to carry my parcels, making a fuss of the child, showing me photos of home.

The market was in the throes of depression, and even the most sullen welcomed this friendly invasion from across the Atlantic as a breath of much-needed hope. Singapore had fallen, Ceylon was being evacuated, India and Australia were threatened. Sisters were without news of brothers, mothers wept silently for their sons last heard of in lands overrun by the Japanese; to those who had no ties and who lacked sensibility, the shortage of tea and rice in the village stores came as a vague, misty foreboding of worse things to come. The newspapers were filled with stories of atrocities in the Far East, of coming cuts in petrol at home which should have been made long before and of utility clothes. There were rumours that coupons would soon be fewer and would purchase less. The new budget was less than a month ahead. Man-power and woman-power were being combed. Shopkeepers were losing their employees; many wondered how long they would be able to keep open. The little milk store in the market's central block put up a notice one morning that it was closing down on quarter day. Soon, we supposed, the shutters of yet other small shops would go up like those of the old curiosity shop that had not opened since that fateful night when bomb blast hurled its African spears and South American saddles into the gutter. Even William Hayward appeared depressed. He spoke of the possibility of closing down the grocery store where his father had made his fortune and his name. The lease was coming to an end and it was questionable, so he declared, whether he would renew it, having only one male assistant left, who might go at any moment. The point was whether he could afford to go on running at a loss. He might even close the cooked-meat shop and the greengrocery store, which were in the same block. Already he was preparing to evacuate the oil shop and transfer it across the road where his crockery establishment had been, but was now being emptied and cleaned for the changeover. I could not imagine the market without Mr Hayward's little string of shops. They seemed an integral part of it. They supplied all our needs. His grocery emporium was a place of rendezvous. The Americans saw in it a reminder of their own hometown general shops where they bought ice-creams and maple sugar. It was the centre of feminine gossip. Priests from nearby Roman Catholic churches arrived with mufflers round their necks carrying huge garden baskets for their provisions. We housewives came for our butter and tea rations, our marmalade and sugar, our porridge and cornflakes. Occasionally one could obtain such rarities as gin and cigarettes, whisky and eggs. The news of some fresh arrival spread through the market as if beaten on the tom-tom, but I never saw a queue, so equally was all this distributed to regular customers. Some unsuspecting housewife, calling for her ration of margarine, would find an egg placed delicately in her shopping basket, and she would hurry away with a smile of satisfaction and her head filled with plans for making a dozen cakes that would surprise a hungry family at tea time.

When night came and enveloped our market in impenetrable darkness under a cold, starlit sky, tinned music came from behind carefully blacked-out windows.

Lady Day passed, and Hayward's grocery store was not closed. We felt quite relieved to hear that some satisfactory arrangement had been made regarding the rent. Perhaps the owners of the property had shown themselves accom-

modating or perhaps William Hayward had felt that it was
his duty to keep the core of his business going for his son,
who was in the army and who might one day wish to carry
on the family tradition. At any rate, the little store continued
to be crowded with shoppers while Mrs Hayward sat
majestically at the cash desk beaming upon her customers
from behind her glass window. It was as if the life of the
market had been reprieved. We breathed more freely and
went about our business with gladdened hearts.

Nevertheless the little milk shop a few doors away closed
its shutters, and Hayward's corner oil shop removed with a
great flourish to the ex-china shop across the road. At the
last moment there had been a great turn-out from basement
to attic, revealing the queerest assortment of goods that had
lain forgotten in dark corners for over forty years. We
inherited, for instance, a piece of toilet soap on the coloured
wrapping of which Victorian horse-drawn omnibuses were
pictured clattering down the Strand, while ladies in long
white dresses, big hats and parasols sauntered along the
pavement. Mr Hayward's oil-shop manager, who had been
in the market for half a century, and who read over and
over again the novels of our neighbour, Elinor Glyn, at
whose feet, I feel sure, he would have laid the contents of
half his shop in return for a smile, supervised the transfer
with humid eyes, like a skipper bidding farewell to his
trusted craft. It was not until he had inspected every corner
of the building, looked under every cobweb, turned over
every piece of yellowed paper, that he finally persuaded
himself to close the front door and turn the key in the lock.

EASTER was the first Sunday in April.

What changes had taken place in Piccadilly Circus during
the last six months? The plinth of Eros was now covered
with yellow and blue posters bearing the words: 'Save in
War Savings.' Underneath the lettering were pictures of
sailors signalling the message with flags.

I stood watching the throb of the Circus a moment from the steps of Swan and Edgar's. There were fourteen other women beside myself waiting for something or somebody on these steps. They had probably said to fourteen men that morning: 'Meet me at the Eros entrance of Swan and Edgar's.' They had all arrived early, or were their menfolk late? It was curious how seldom one ever saw a man waiting on these steps. Perhaps as a sex they are not as patient as we are. Next to me was a girl in a pink woollen coat with a sprig of white heather in the lapel. She wore a small blue hat decorated with blue and red ostrich feathers, and it was perched becomingly over one eye. Now and again she would nervously clutch her big handbag and scan the crowd surging round the Circus.

Behind us the big shop window had paper crocuses growing from green matting amongst the gloves and stockings. At the entrance to the underground the newspaper sellers, with their backs against the square brick police shelter on the kerb, were crying out the evening papers. On the other side of the Circus, between Etam and Shaftesbury Avenue, and below the huge Guinness clock, the empty shop, where the preceding month collections were made for Warship Week, was now taken over by the Ministry of Food to teach housewives how to make the best of the new national flour.

In another forty-eight hours the white loaf was to disappear until the end of the war. The significance of this momentous decision had not yet quite dawned upon the public. They had taken the white loaf for granted during two and a half years of war. Most of this time we were the only nation in Europe to enjoy this inestimable privilege. We could buy as much white bread as we liked while people on the Continent queued up for a black substitute. Some, like the Spaniards and the Greeks, had not bread at all. Even now we were not to be pitied, for the national flour, though no longer white, was perfectly good, though there was no telling what the future might bring.

Outside the shop where the lessons for housewives were being given was displayed a huge coloured canvas portraying an Atlantic convoy with the words:

'National Flour Saves Shipping.'

An official began to test a loudspeaker, which suddenly blared out so hoarsely that there was a momentary jerk in the traffic as drivers wondered where the noise came from.

Only one of the women whose group I had joined was gone. The girl with the sprig of heather gave a suppressed cry of joy as a soldier emerged from the passing crowd to lead her away by the arm.

I crossed over to Etam in the hope of finding some stockings but I was told to come back in three days' time. Displayed both in the window and on the counter was lingerie in delicate blues and pinks, and by the cash desk a bowl of 'flowers' cut out of crêpe de Chine. Our stockings and slips were not yet made of nylon—that was to be a dream of the future.

The doors of the Monico swung incessantly as the eighteen-penny afternoon tea crowd dived in and out. There was a huge queue at the Eros News Reel Theatre where there were shots from the Far East; another queue at the cooked-meat bar, with a milk churn at the door (this was on the other side of Shaftesbury Avenue); and yet another queue outside the London Pavilion, then a picture house with only one's memory to recall the days when Charles B. Cochran's revues flashed the names of their stars from blinding electric signs across the full width of the famous theatre.

A great sea of people stretched away towards Leicester Square. The cinemas, the theatres, the sandwich bars and the fun-fair were crowded. One had to move slowly, threading a zigzag path amongst these human breakers overflowing the pavements. A Japanese, the corners of whose hard-set mouth seemed to suggest a faintly ironic smile, pursued his way through the heart of our empire at death grips with the Land of the Rising Sun. A policeman followed two paces behind. Londoners were now accustomed to the sight of these Japanese diplomats out walking with a police escort.

EVEN in war time there were ghosts of the past to be found in this great and noble city. There were memories to remind us of what life was like before the war, and to warn us that things would be different afterwards.

There were ghosts in Clarence House one sunny afternoon when the green lawn that was common to the whole of St James's Palace was girdled with golden daffodils. The Duke of Connaught, the last of Queen Victoria's sons, had died, and the auctioneers had been plastering what they liked to call the 'remaining contents' of his London house with numbered tabs to coincide with the items on the catalogue, preparatory to the sale the following morning.

Half a dozen bowler-hatted, professional dealers with blasé expressions put down a shilling each for a catalogue at the lodge, and passed silently under the glass portico overlooking the gardens. I was not the only woman but most of the others had come in country tweeds. One or two courtiers were also paying their respects to a passing regime. It was all rather melancholy and funereal. One wondered vaguely what would happen to this house that had changed occupants only three times during its one hundred and thirty years of existence. Built for William IV when he was Duke of Clarence, the house remained his residence for some time after he became King. Queen Victoria then gave it to her mother, the Duchess of Kent, who lived there until she died in 1861. Five years later it passed to the Queen's second son, the Duke of Edinburgh, who largely remodelled it, building the portico overlooking the garden. Its next occupant was the Duke of Connaught, the successive tenures of the two brothers lasting exactly three quarters of a century.

There were crimson carpets on the stairs and in the halls,

but the pictures, or what was left of them, were stacked in heaps on the floor. The reception rooms on the ground floor, where some of the windows had suffered badly from blast, were filled with massive mahogany furniture of the mid-Victorian period, though on the first floor there were some lighter rooms furnished in imitation French Empire style. There was a semicircular settee in one room, on which nearly a dozen people could sit. I think our grandmothers called it a 'sociable'. It was upholstered in white and yellow.

One would have thought that the reception rooms would have overlooked the garden with its sweeping lawn and distant view of the Mall and St James's Park—a regal view for a royal residence—but they all overlooked the street. I crossed over to the bedrooms, expecting such airiness as would take my breath away. I imagined our late soldier-duke waking in the morning to survey from his canopied bed a truly pastoral scene, while in June he sniffed the freshly mown grass that the Office of Works trundled away in a horse-drawn cart for hay. His royal highness's bed was an old iron affair, and the windows were so boxed up that it was well-nigh impossible to see out of them. There was a highly incommodious prehistoric bathroom, partitioned off at the back, with no access whatever to light or air. In a corner I found a stack of children's toys—a rocking horse, some toy trains and a banjolele—which the catalogue cruelly described as 'sundry games'. There were three easels and a brand-new topee or pith helmet, the brim lined with green satin, thrown into a box with a collection of tired lampshades. Who had owned the musical box and the Victorian cane-backed child's chair? Who stepped into a royal carriage with that parasol with the lacquer handle I was tempted to buy? From what eastern land came this yellow silk kimono? What might be the story of that malacca cane with the ivory top?

Ten days after Easter one might have seen a small para-

graph in *The Times* announcing that the surplus contents of
Wimborne House were to be sold by auction early in May.
Here indeed were ghosts in plenty. One might safely say
that Wimborne House was one of the very last of the big
London mansions where both political and social entertaining took place on a grand scale. I had on several occasions been a guest in this rather squat and rambling house
which is next to, and under the shadow of, the Ritz Hotel.
The great french windows of the big drawing-room overlooked the Green Park, but the entrance was through the
courtyard in Arlington Street, where at night a linkman in
livery and top hat swung his dim lantern as he opened
carriage doors. On entering the marble hall one heard the
screeching of multi-coloured parakeets kept beside the
fountain by Alice Lady Wimborne. All the big reception
rooms were on the ground floor, opening one into the
other. There was the Italian ballroom, with its rather over-
powering red and gold Genoese velvet hangings, a room
lit at night by unshaded candles in four large lustres, which
gave forth eerie flickers and great heat. A sixteenth-century
stone fireplace came from Blois.

A few Londoners still remembered Cornelia Lady Wimborne, the great Liberal hostess, whose parties in late
Victorian days were so famous. Her son, the late Lord
Wimborne, continued the Liberal tradition, and up to a
few years earlier Wimborne House had been the scene of a
Liberal reception on the eve of the opening of Parliament,
just as Londonderry House staged a similar reception for
the Conservative Party.

Lord Wimborne did not make the house his home on
succeeding to the title, but his father used almost every day
to walk into the Ritz for lunch, where he occupied the same
corner table in lonely glory. It was said that César Ritz once
wished to enlarge his hotel and wrote to his neighbour,
offering to buy Wimborne House, whereupon Lord Wimborne answered:

'My home is not in the market, but as I am thinking of

enlarging my garden, perhaps you will consider selling me the Ritz?'

As THE R.A.F. spring offensive over Germany gathered strength the Luftwaffe sought vengeance on our cathedral cities of Bath, Exeter and Norwich. London continued to enjoy its uneasy respite, and the life of the capital throbbed faster than ever. Polyglot crowds swirled round Piccadilly Circus; restaurant owners, busier than ever, augmented their menus with roast rook, bought champagne at three pounds a bottle hoping to re-sell it as twice the price, and vaguely wondered how their businesses would fare when the Government fixed a maximum price for meals. Theatrical first-nights followed one another, and though we no longer wore evening gowns or ermine wraps, the men made up for our lack of splendour by being nearly all in uniform. London was reaching out after the feverishness that characterized it in 1917. It was now a whole year since the last devastating air raid, and even the worst scars had healed with the passing of time. Thousands of children had come back from the country, and in Piccadilly Circus one saw on occasion a couple of red-capped military policewomen giving a helping hand to some urchin wheeling a perambulator across the street. People were beginning to take a topsy-turvy world for granted. Warm, sunlit days suddenly covered trees with green foliage, and Londoners found themselves on the threshold of another summer with nothing particular to look forward to but separation from their loved ones, no holidays, more air raids or perhaps invasion.

THE INCREDIBLE CITY

THE INCREDIBLE CITY

SEPTEMBER was half over, but the Western Gateway of the Mediterranean still glittered in hot sunshine. The sea, between the African and Spanish mainlands, reflected the deep blue of a cloudless sky. On the opposing fringes of both continents a long, rainless summer had dried the earth and shrivelled the flowers, but the orange and lemon trees were heavy with fruit, not yet gold but a deep green, and the thick-skinned pomegranates, growing in orchards like apples, had reached maturity.

The secret of the coming Allied landing in French North Africa was too well guarded for the slightest rumour to be carried by the hot, damp Levanter about the great Armada that was marshalling its forces in northern waters. Nevertheless there was a feeling of restless expectancy, and people spoke in hushed tones of the last epic convoy that had smashed its way through to Malta. There were stories of heroism recounted in the bar of the Rock Hotel in Gibraltar. The highlights of the drama reached one by ricochet. There were heroes who shook their heads knowingly, survivors from lost ships, and battered grey monsters steaming into Gibraltar by night.

The sun had reached midday strength, and tied up to the mole was a ship ready to return to England. She was a curious shape, squat amidships, fast-looking but quite small. Her time of sailing was a secret, but smoke was rising from her funnels and her decks were crowded, while motor-cars sped along the mole making for her gangway. Officially the ship had no name but those who had seen her before recognized her as a cross-channel steamer which in the days of peace plied between Liverpool and Dublin. The needs of war had sent this little ship far off of her course, just as the beaches of Dunkirk once beckoned to barges that had previously never sailed farther than the Thames Estuary.

A unit of a famous British regiment was returning to England on the ship. The men had been on board since the previous day. Just now some Allied officers, some foreign civilians and a few women and children were coming up the gangway. There were also half a dozen young pilot officers from Malta, wearing on their tunics small Maltese crosses that they had cut out of metal. The narrow promenade deck, on which anti-aircraft guns were mounted, was crowded with soldiers in shorts. There was a tremendous bustle that suggested imminent departure and the women retired to their cabins to be out of the way until they knew for certain whether the ship would leave that evening.

The cabins were clean but small. The women were quartered amidships and there were as many nationalities as amongst the men. The young woman returning to England alone smiled shyly at the Polish women of whom there were about a dozen, some of them with children, all, so they told her, on the last lap of a journey that had taken them more than three years, travelling unhappily from country to country. Two Frenchwomen had arrived mysteriously out of Occupied France. One, red-haired and slim, her rather wan features enlivened by the irrepressible vitality of Parisians even in time of war, was in the middle thirties. The other, scarcely more than twenty, pretty and fresh, was from a small town in Brittany and appeared as silent as her companion was talkative.

Not long after dusk two tenders sidled up to starboard, and ropes were thrown down. The cross-channel steamer began to move gently out of harbour into the violet waters of a Mediterranean dotted here and there with the lights of Spanish fishing smacks close to the mountainous coast. One could sense great relief throughout the ship at her prompt departure. However circuitous the route, whatever dangers lay ahead, all the people were now on their way to England.

At breakfast the next morning most of the civilians found themselves at a long table at the head of which sat the ship's adjutant, a colonel with iron grey hair, whose momentary worry was how to deal with a soldier caught smoking on deck during the night. A cigarette can reveal the presence of a ship to a submarine and was a serious offence. Great chunks of pure white bread stood on plates along the centre of the table, and the menu consisted of porridge, fried fish, eggs and bacon, and toast and marmalade. The prodigality of this fare overwhelmed one of the Polish women whose lean fingers caressed the bread as if she were unable to believe that it was real. The passengers had brought their lifebelts into the dining-room and the women were taught by the men how to hang the unwieldy things over the backs of their chairs.

The weather was warm, and from time to time the naval engineer, looking out of the porthole next to which he sat, pointed out a school of porpoises playing in the water.

After breakfast the young woman went up on the narrow promenade deck to get some air and watch the distant coastline. A Sunderland was circling round in a friendly way and the captain, an Irishman, who saw nothing incongruous in approving De Valera politically while he himself sailed the Seven Seas in the service of the British, came up to talk to her. He had taken his ship three times to Dunkirk, evacuated our nationals from Bordeaux and made innumerable trips across the Atlantic and to Iceland.

The passengers had no idea yet of the route or how long they would take, but the rumour was that the ship would strike due west, well beyond the Azores, before turning north, and those who had brought no warm clothing wondered if indeed they might not make a detour by Canada before reaching England. The ship was soon escorted by a destroyer that zigzagged in front like a hound following a lost scent. A little knot of Italian prisoners, strangely garbed, some wearing cotton nightcaps with peaked ends that flopped over the right ear, stood watching it.

On the first evening because the weather remained calm, the passengers started to make friends. Most of the men had been in at least one concentration camp either in Europe or in Northern Africa, and all had learned that languages were no real barrier. The Lady of Paris held salon in the lounge. The Breton girl sat beside her but seldom opened her mouth. People admired her modesty and the fact that anybody so frail and, in appearance, so naïve, could have made a journey across Europe, enduring perils and hardships that only the bravest men were willing to face. It was a point of honour that no passenger should question another about the way that she or he had escaped from bondage but this did not prevent occasional bursts of confidence. On one of the rare occasions when the Breton girl spoke it was to describe, in that gentle, childish voice, how on a summer morning one of her companions, while hiding from the Germans in the branches of a cherry tree, saw a young Nazi officer swing himself on to an adjoining branch to pick some of the ripe fruit.

'The officer seemed surprised,' said the Breton girl, 'and asked in broken French whether my companion lived close by, to which, of course, he answered as convincingly as possible. They became quite friendly.'

'Yes,' put in a tall, lanky Belgian whose fierce moustaches made him look like a modern D'Artagnan, 'one must never lose one's nerve.'

'The most terrifying moment I ever had', he continued, 'was one morning in Paris when I turned into the Rue Royale. The trouble about the streets of Paris since the German Occupation is that they are so confoundedly empty, and a man as tall as I cannot expect to walk down an empty street without attracting more attention than is good for him when he is in hiding. I had not proceeded half way down before a compatriot turned into the street from the Rue St Honoré and, recognizing me, started to wave his arms, shouting: "Why, I'm blessed if it isn't my old friend Charles! How long have you been in Paris? We must have dinner together." "Impossible," I answered, trying to put a stop to his ill-timed effusions; "I am returning to Brussels this evening." "Then we must have a drink immediately. I shall take you to Maxim's where they still have a little brandy because those 'gentlemen' like to foregather there." "You are very kind but I have an appointment." "An appointment?" echoed this crashing bore, "then you must allow me to accompany you on your way, so that, at least, we can have ten minutes to talk about old times.""

'I wonder what has happened to my flat in Paris?' put in the Lady of the Red Hair, with a laugh that showed how little she really minded. 'What troubles me most is that I was obliged to leave a dozen new hats behind, and I need not tell any of you who have been in Paris lately how becoming are the hats this season, all trimmed with tulle and flowers. And that reminds me to ask if flats are difficult to obtain in London and what are the most fashionable hat shops?'

She had turned to the young woman as the only person capable of giving her this information, and with a pencil poised over her notebook was waiting for the answer.

'I am afraid you will find that few of us wear pretty hats any longer. Most of us manage with a snood or a silk square, but I have a friend who owns a hat shop in Berkeley Square . . .'

'Oh well,' she said, 'we'll talk about that later.' She put her notebook and pencil back in her handbag. 'Heavens! Look at this!' she exclaimed. 'I brought a piece of Paris bread away with me as a souvenir. Feel its weight, as heavy as stone, and yet I was often tempted to eat it during my journey. I am afraid the white bread they offer us on board ship will give me indigestion before I get used to it.'

'I suffer less from white bread than from mental reaction,' said a young Belgian surgeon called Scissors because of the sharpness of his voice. 'One becomes so accustomed to fighting back in the Occupied Countries that I find it almost irksome to realize that one is no longer surrounded by enemies.'

As he spoke the ship gave a sudden lurch and the glasses were thrown on the floor.

'The gods heard you!' boomed Charles. 'Perhaps the enemy is nearer than you think.'

There had been an anxious silence but soon the familiar drone of the engine was heard again as the steamer ploughed forward. Somebody came into the lounge by the starboard door which put out all the lights. This often happened and caused a chorus of invective, because each time the door was opened the lights were extinguished automatically to prevent the promenade deck from being lit up. The new arrival was the Parisian's fifteen-year-old daughter, a girl with expressive eyes and short, dark hair. For the benefit of the men who had not yet made her acquaintance, the Lady of Paris said: 'This is my daughter.' She added: 'I fear she is incorrigible. Though she has not been on board ship for much longer than twenty-four hours she has already flirted with half the officers of the regiment. If her spirits are turbulent, you must put that down to reaction after her adventures, for when we were in danger she showed herself both calm and discreet. The most terrible danger is in those homes where patriots are hidden. The game is for high stakes. Death is the punishment, and that is a hard school for little girls.'

'We men', said Charles, 'leave a letter for our young wives, telling them that we have run away with another woman. That is the only way. The Gestapo arrives and asks the housewife: "Where is your husband? Has he left for England?" and then the wife, with unfeigned tears, shows the letter.'

'But how do we know', put in Scissors, 'that sometimes

our wives do not really believe that we have run away with another woman? What do they think when the days turn into weeks, and the weeks into months and years, and never a single word?'

'And what', went on Charles, 'can our wives tell our children? Do they say that their fathers are living in adultery? Are they forced to say so?'

The ship was beginning to toss and by the following day there would doubtless be no more flying fishes. The young woman decided to go to her cabin and at the foot of the stairs met the captain who was doubtless on his way to the bridge. She told him she supposed he had little time for sleep. 'I can do with two hours' sleep in twenty-four,' he said to her in his thick Irish brogue, 'and as it is my belief that doing without sleep is a matter of habit, I allow myself no more than that when I am at home on leave.' This theory sounded hard on his wife.

The sea became rougher during the night and the next day the passengers woke to grey skies, but on deck though windy it was not cold. The slightly colder weather and the sea air were wonderfully invigorating after the heat of the Mediterranean. The destroyer was still engaged in her feverish crisscross motions. Sometimes she would hare off at full speed as if suddenly on the scent of a submarine but would then after investigation come back and resume her antics. The young woman was joined by the Lady of Paris and after they had talked for a moment, a rather cadaverous-looking Frenchman came up to pass the time of day. He had apparently lived for the last five years in Casablanca where finally his pro-British sympathies had made him suspect. He was a schoolmaster and became very heated on what he considered was the most urgent task in his profession—to reorganize the school and university curriculum! Indeed he became so excited that, menacing the two women with his forefinger, he exclaimed: 'Are you willing to face up to this all-important matter?' Their lack of enthusiasm made

him move away sullenly, his bony fingers gripping the
ribbons of his life-jacket: 'Women are never alive to the
fundamentals of life,' he muttered. The moment was
doubtless ill-chosen but perhaps he was a crank twenty
years ahead of his time.

The destroyer had made another of her impetuous dashes
—this time to port—as if sensing a hidden danger. Then
she quivered with excitement. Suddenly she dropped a
depth bomb, the vibrations of which hit the steel plates of
the small vessel, causing it to bump like a cork. There was
another explosion and then a third during which the cross-
channel steamer continued to cut through the water without changing course, so that soon it had left its escort well
behind where she was circling, like a dog chasing its tail.
A few moments later she decided to resume her position
ahead and now rushed back at full steam. As she came
abreast, looking magnificent with her bows hidden in spray,
she seemed to sing out proudly: 'What do you know about
that?' If the passengers loved her before, they certainly
loved her twice as fondly now.

An unassuming young man was talking to the Lady of
Paris. 'We arrived in Berlin at 8 a.m.,' he was saying. Simple
words but most intriguing. He was telling her how he had
escaped from a prisoner-of-war camp in Prussia with two
other Belgians. On arrival in Berlin, they needed to change
the Belgian francs their comrades had given them before
their escape. They saw a Cambio. It was a terrible risk but
the young man went up to the official and asked him in very
bad German if he would change the money. The man
answered: 'Of course. How do you like working in Germany? I see in the papers that over a thousand Belgian
workers are reaching Germany every week. You're very
lucky to be posted in Berlin.'

What a band of intrepid adventurers had gathered together on this ship. There was not one of these foreigners
but had risked his or her life to reach London—that magic
city which shone like a torch over Europe in bondage.

Charles, on being asked what he wanted to do most on arrival, said: 'To see where the voice of the B.B.C. comes from. Night after night our people listen to that voice as if it were an oracle. It is even picked up in the prison camps in Spain and disseminated by the priests at confession.'

As the weather became colder, the officers discarded their shorts for battledress. The problem was not so easily solved for the Breton girl who owned nothing but the little cotton dress in which she had travelled from Brittany to the southernmost tip of Spain, and though her cabin friends came to her rescue she was mostly to be seen pacing the deck in a sailor's dark-blue woollen sweater under oilskins. As finally the ship came into line with the Brittany coast (though at least five hundred miles to the west of it), the Breton girl looked across the ocean with tears in her eyes. From a little port on that rocky promontory, far beyond the horizon, she had tried to escape in a fishing smack, but too many of her compatriots had slipped away during the hours of darkness, and on the night she had planned to leave the Germans closed the bay with a girdle of fast motor boats which, at the slightest sound, were ready to light up the water with powerful arc-lamps. It was for this reason that she chose the longer route. She had succeeded where so many had failed, but just then she was a young girl dreaming of her home and her parents, and with every throb of the engine she was being taken farther away from them.

While she was thus straining her eyes eastwards, the young woman came upon her and, guessing what was in her mind, respected her silence. There was a light breeze that blew their hair about but the sea was wonderfully calm, and it must have been in the late afternoon, for the sun was approaching the end of its course. Suddenly the Breton girl uttered a little cry and, pointing to the horizon where it was just possible to make out a curious square sail reddish-brown in colour, exclaimed: 'That's a Brittany tunny fisher!' Slowly the beautiful vessel came near enough to be seen in all her glory, and then the destroyer, very majestically and making a graceful curve, went out to meet her. It really seemed as if these Brittany sailors had come a thousand miles to bid farewell to their young compatriot. The destroyer thought it wise to make inquiries, for harmless-looking fishing smacks were often used by the Germans to act as decoys for their submarines off the French coast. The destroyer let down a boat, which was rowed out to the sailing ship, and a man behind the two women said: 'They've probably gone to see if she carries a wireless set. Perhaps they'll take the crew off and sink her by gunfire. That ought to be good fun to watch!' The Breton girl trembled at these words.

The cross-channel steamer had halted and the young woman thought it strange to be riding the water so silently without the throb of an engine. Half an hour later the party of bluejackets returned to the destroyer which slowly steamed away, the channel steamer in her wake, engines purring once more. The tunny vessel sailed into the sinking sun and soon she was nothing but a speck on the horizon.

The captain was to have a touch of the same homesickness as the girl. He said it happened to him each time he approached the shores of Eire: 'And who knows that if we were to be shipwrecked off Dublin, I would not to be washed ashore and locked up as a belligerent!' This idea made him beam with pleasure.

Now at last, after a concert on the last evening which Charles compèred, the passengers were approaching their journey's end. The Lady of Paris was thinking of her husband who was due to leave France by a much more dangerous route. His real name was not known to any on board. Scissors was a surgeon who had studied under Martel, the French surgeon who opened his veins when he saw the Nazis marching up the Champs-Elysées in June 1940. Charles, who had been at Miranda, the Spanish concentration camp north of Madrid, was a journalist. The Polish women were praying that they would be reunited

with their menfolk whom they had not seen since the rape
of Poland. All were keyed up to the point of fanaticism.

On Sunday morning the passengers looking through
their portholes before breakfast could see the undulating
green hills of Ayr. What tender colouring this pasture land
seemed to have after the burnt-up brown of the Mediterranean coast! Now and again they passed a troopship lying
at anchor in mid stream and occasionally a Catalina would
fly low above them. Now they were in the Clyde. Thousands
of Americans had looked upon this picture after crossing the
Atlantic, most of them for the first time, to take part in the
war. By midday the ship had dropped anchor in the river
with other ships behind and in front. The captain, the
R.A.F. pilots from Malta, the diplomat and the young
woman were allowed to go ashore in the tender which
landed them beside a railway station of a small branch line
where the next train was not due out for two hours. Everything here was under the influence of a sleepy Sunday
afternoon but there were Sunday papers, American officers
in comfortable armchairs beside tables groaning under
home-made scones in the lounge of the small hotel. The
young woman was sad to have been parted from the Lady
of Paris, the Breton girl and the Belgian journalist, Charles,
who all had to be vetted by the authorities; sad to leave
the gallant little ship that had brought them all safely to
Britain at war; but her thoughts already preceded her to
London where she wondered if things had changed much
since she was last there.

THE traffic in the West End had probably diminished but it
seemed extraordinarily dense to anybody who had seen the
dearth of petrol-driven cars on the Continent. Londoners
were complaining that taxis were hard to find and one of
the effects of scarcer petrol was the long line of buses that
during the middle of the day stood idle in Hyde Park. Even
so one still had to pick a safe moment to cross Piccadilly

and we had not yet, as in Madrid, returned to the age of the buggy cart and the two-in-hand, or, as in Paris, to a few bicycles and an occasional bus brought out of a museum and drawn by a couple of ill-fed horses. Mr May still drove his business cab for a Bond Street hatter, but this was mere conservatism, for Mr May had driven the same cab through the streets of London for the last thirty years.

London had become fuller, and the thousands of children evacuated during the raids were now back. It was practically impossible for a stranger to find a flat, and in nearly all the large blocks owners were putting up rents. The hotels were so full that many people, who because of their business had to spend a week in Town, were obliged to sleep every night in a different hotel. The shops were still richly stocked with merchandise—there were chocolate cakes and buns at the pastry-cooks' and violets and roses at the florists'; the bread was almost white and so plentiful that people who arrived from the Continent could not believe it.

Londoners were still smarting under the fall of Tobruk, however, and less confident than were those who had seen the work of the Navy in the Mediterranean. The restaurants were so crowded that it was often necessary to book a table a day in advance. The law had laid down a maximum price for meals, but because of certain additional charges according to the class of the restaurant the result was to increase prices, though only slightly.

Shepherd Market was now known as Eisenhower Platz because of the growing number of American troops who frequented it. The Americans, whose clubs and hostels were all round us, gathered in the evening at Shepherd's, the rather superior public house in Hertford Street which, from the summer of 1940 onwards, had become a rendezvous for fighter pilots in the Battle of Britain. The manager was a man called Oscar who was very proud of his young clientele. He was in charge of the fire-fighting squad that every Saturday night gathered in the basement of Carrington House while the roof-spotters, all tenants of the building, patrolled the roof. Though I went up occasionally to gossip with Elinor Glyn's maid or the great novelist herself in her strange apartment I was excused from both roof-spotting and fire-fighting on the grounds that I had a baby. This did not prevent me from paying short visits to Oscar's group of market people who, in the case of an emergency, were supposed to hurry off with a trailer pump to put out the fires signalled from above. I thus unwittingly fell amongst a band of publicans which was strange because I never once went into a local pub of which we had a full quota. In addition to Shepherd's there were the Bunch of Grapes, the King's Arms, the Old Chesterfield and the King and Queen in Brick Street. The men and women from these establishments liked to do their fire-fighting on the same night and had elected Oscar to be their chief. Their solidarity was entirely professional. Though they signed the book at dusk, they carried on behind their respective bars, unless there was an alert, when they left their clients to fend for themselves. Soon after 11 p.m. they dropped into the guardroom, put on rubber boots and tin hats and, having inspected the stirrup pumps and water-pails, took out the equipment for a drill.

At this point I received an invitation from the Lady of Paris to a dinner party in her apartment at Grosvenor House. I was already aware that a good deal of mystery surrounded her real identity—or to be more precise the identity of her husband, who was said to be the most intrepid and colourful of those secret agents organizing the resistance movement in France and who, by virtue of their activities, were dropped over occupied territory, making their way back as best they could. Pierre's arrival was awaited with great anxiety by the authorities in London who had important and delicate work for him to perform. The Lady of Paris had become a legendary figure in her own right and I had become so accustomed to thinking of her as a feminine Scarlet Pimpernel crossing mountains and rivers in a light grey coat and skirt that I was rather taken aback to find her so elegantly dressed and so much at ease in this London hotel. Many of that small group thrown together during their picturesque journey from Gibraltar seemed at first a trifle shy. Charles discussed the latest films in town as if he had never been to Miranda. I even wondered if some of the guests might in this different atmosphere be a little suspicious of one another. The Breton girl who, unlike Charles, had not been to the cinema since her arrival in London, discussed the German films she had seen in France. However, one did hear echoes of what these people had talked about on the ship. When, for instance, a young Belgian whom the guests called the Millionaire was being congratulated for leaving a wife and four young children behind in order to come to England to enlist as an airman in the R.A.F., he exclaimed: 'I am not a brave man. Scissors over there is a brave man. He risked his life a dozen times to get patriots and British aviators out of Belgium. He was caught once just as he was stepping out of a country lane to keep a rendezvous with an aeroplane and was tortured, but he escaped through France and Spain and swam six miles to Gibraltar on a pitch dark night. The Breton girl is brave, for she is a mere girl and has nerves of steel. The Lady of Paris is brave, for she brought two children out of France by a route that is even more dangerous than any of us took, and as for her husband—well, he jumps into boiling water, knowing what it is to be scalded.'

The talk went on along these lines until fairly late in the night when suddenly a small dark-haired man broke into the room. 'Come,' said the Lady of Paris to me: 'let me introduce you to my husband!' That was my first sight of Pierre whose subsequent exploits and appalling death were to write his name into history.

Personally I found a tremendous exhilaration at finding myself in Town. The news had suddenly become good. Towards three o'clock on the afternoon of Friday 6th

November the evening newspaper sellers in Regent Street chalked red, white and blue frames round posters announcing that Rommel's panzers were in flight out of Egypt. There was an effervescence that could be felt rather than seen. I walked down Burlington Street into Bond Street where a young A.T.S. with a service gas-mask slung over a shoulder was clasping a baby as she hurried on her way. A few yards farther on a bluejacket, accompanied by a distinguished-looking man with a beard whom I took to be his father, stopped in front of an art gallery, exclaiming: 'That looks like a Munnings!' People stopped to peer into the windows of small jewellers', where their interest was roused in gold trinkets, many Victorian, which were offered as safe investments against inflation. The National Fire Service sump in Bond Street was decorated with posters advertising the Greek Exhibition at Burlington House. The following day, after a morning of heavy rain, the sun came out and I wheeled my baby in the pram down Kensington Palace Gardens which in pre-war days was known as Millionaires' Row. In peace time most of these mid-Victorian mansions were owned by bankers, shipping magnates and maharajahs, and the countrified avenue in which they stood was nominally closed at both ends and policed by a porter wearing an impressive uniform with gold buttons and a tall silk hat. There was a pathetic emptiness about the palaces of the rich and the gardens were running wild. A couple of army lorries stopped in front of a deserted mansion, and out of them tumbled a bevy of girls in khaki who started to drag palliasses across the lawn, tossing them through the open french windows of what must once have been somebody's ballroom. On the other side of the road the Red Flag flew above the Soviet Embassy for the twenty-fifth anniversary of the Soviet Republic. The garden was bare except for a few red geraniums, some holly berries and a child's tricycle that lay in the centre of a gravel path. The tricycle was red too. A car swept into the drive, and a woman, clasping a great bunch of deep red roses, ran up the steps leading to the front door, which was immediately opened. Her action personified the desire of the whole nation to pay tribute to Russian resistance.

I tried in the middle of London at war to lead a normally feminine existence. I made the beds, cooked the meals, queued up at the shops and took my baby out in the pram for long walks. The backcloth against which I did these things was, of course, far from normal. I laid out lunch every day on the big round cherrywood table in the living room. The two large windows, which no longer had any glass in them, only some sort of black material, were always wide open and as they gave directly on to the courtyard, low enough to be easily looked into from outside, anybody who wished to could drop in to share our meal. The baby in his tall chair was the great attraction. Men who had left their own families behind to cross half Europe in order to continue the war were starved for this one thing I could offer them, the chatter of a woman and the babbling of a gay, amusing baby. I never found myself short of plain, wholesome food. The erudite head of a cypher department, a man so learned that one had the impression he had swallowed the contents of the *Encyclopaedia Britannica*, invariably brought me his food tickets, as so many others did, and these I translated into shoulders of lamb and steak and kidney pies. My pekinese completed the family atmosphere. There were occasions when men who had been dropped on foreign soil, in Belgium, in Holland, in France, came back unexpectedly bringing some trifling gift, the leaves of a foreign tree, a flower, a packet of cigarettes, an ear of corn which filled us all with wonderment. I tried hard to prevent them from talking. Such secrets should not have been for feminine ears.

The news that the Allies had landed in Algiers and at Oran was announced over the radio at seven on a radiant Sunday morning. That morning I walked through Hyde Park. The

Daisy Walk was almost deserted, but the grass was still green and there were chrysanthemums in the flower-beds by the Row. Wire netting stood between the path and the Dell, from which the rabbits had disappeared, probably because rabbit pie is an enviable dish in war time. The bridge spanning the extreme end of the Serpentine now stood over dry land. Its Victorian lamp-posts had been battered by bombs. Part of the Serpentine was reclaimed, giving, in the white November mist, a fen-country effect, with gulls and waterfowl on the flat surface of the new land. The filling up of this end of the lake was to prevent water rushing down into Knightsbridge were a lucky bomb to fall on the crest of the hill.

On the north side of the lake a small crowd was feeding the ducks; on the south side there was a line of fishermen. Fishing in the Serpentine was not allowed in peace time. The anglers now sat on canvas chairs, their eyes fixed on the floats bobbing up and down in the leaf-strewn water. The right to fish in the lake had been given to them as compensation for not using the railways. Before the war one would have found them at Pangbourne, at Appleford and at Culham.

My village in Piccadilly had changed little during the last six months except that more and more Americans were to be seen in the streets. They called to each other with strange Red Indian war cries and organized baseball games in the Green Park. They were terribly generous, distributing packets of American cigarettes and chewing-gum. They were most particular about their appearance, and their trousers were perfectly pressed. Their hostels and clubs were augmenting in number, especially between Grosvenor Square and Piccadilly, and it was a long cry from the days when, before the United States entered the war, a small bunch of American Marines was sent over to serve as fire-guards at the U.S. Embassy, with orders to change into civilian dress when off duty. The first uniformed troops were housed in two Piccadilly buildings—the former Hotel Splendide and the Badminton Club. Others were billeted near the Embassy in Grosvenor Square. Then began a pincer movement converging on our market; South Audley Street became a miniature Fifth Avenue, the late Sir Philip Sassoon's palatial mansion facing Stanhope Gate became a Senior U.S. Officers' Club, and the Washington Hotel in Curzon Street blossomed out as the American Red Cross Washington Club for doughboys. Meanwhile Half Moon Street and Clarges Street, famous in the old days for aristocratic bachelor lodgings, became an American dormitory. There was not a tailor, a shoemaker, a laundry, or a French cleaner in our market that did not start working overtime to cope with this invasion. They hammered and sewed, they ironed and washed, all day and far into the night. Prosperity had burst upon them.

Thanksgiving Day was the first solemn occasion that the Americans celebrated since they had arrived in force. After services at Westminster Abbey and Westminster Cathedral, a lunch was held at the Junior Officers' Mess. The turkeys which should have been eaten were generously handed over to hospitals; instead the menu consisted of soup, celery, mixed pickles, roast loin of pork and apple fritters, mashed potatoes, sweet corn, apple and celery salad, and plum pudding. In the evening there was a dance at the Washington Club to which many of the young women in the market, myself included, were invited. It was a dark night and two tall sergeants directed traffic through the swing doors to prevent guests from passing too precipitously from the night into the brilliantly lit interior. These swing doors led one from the heart of London into another life. One had the impression of crossing within the space of a few seconds the broad Atlantic. American accents, from the New York twang to the drawl of the Southern States, replaced the warm, slow talk of the London streets. There was a faint but appetizing smell of apple tart and cream, roast pork and Camel cigarettes. The newspaper racks were

Mr Hayward's greengrocery

The oil shop

filled with journals from every State of the Union, and the
familiar red postbox was replaced by a U.S. army mailbag.
An entire wall was covered with posters of the New York
Central and Southern Pacific railroads. In a corridor was a
huge map of America on which were scribbled in pencil
thousands of names and addresses. The idea was that each
man should write his name as near as possible to his hometown, inviting others to get in touch with him. In a huge
room with plain white walls we danced the boogie-woogie,
the conga and the samba, we girls deliriously happy to be
so few amongst so many men. In a corner silver machines
were turning out hundreds of doughnuts spread with
powdered sugar.

The Breton girl came to lunch the following Sunday, and
indeed from then on she was constantly in the apartment,
helping me in the kitchen, coming with me when I took the
baby out in the pram, joining our small group of women
in what we called the drawing-room of the Green Park.
She was entirely changed after her long rest—extremely pretty
with her golden hair and large, expressive eyes. She wore a
neatly tailored grey coat and skirt and was no longer the
silent, homesick girl I remembered but was gay and expan-
sive. The Lady of Paris's husband had once referred to her
as the Angel of Brittany and this appellation kept on coming
back into my mind as she told me by degrees her incredible
trek across Europe.

She had taken a small flat in Chelsea, and after we had put
Bobby to bed that evening, I accompanied her as far as the
bus stop at Hyde Park Corner. It was one of those dark
nights that seemed to take one back to the Middle Ages.
The streets were almost deserted, though from time to time
one saw the glow of an electric torch making dim circles
on the pavement in front of hurrying feet, while the tall
lamp-posts with their pinprick lights cast fantastic shadows
on the darkened buildings. We turned down Hamilton
Place into Piccadilly, passing the house in which the future

Queen Elizabeth was born and which during the night raids was partly destroyed by a bomb that covered me with dust and rubble as I was about to wheel my pram across the road.

The coffee stall opposite St George's Hospital was still functioning and as we came level with it a girl, very slight of build, stood behind the counter with a cup of tea in her gloved hand. 'George,' she was saying to the white-coated attendant, 'you haven't given me a lump of sugar.' To which George answered: 'I put sugar in tea when I'm asked for it—not otherwise.' As there was no bus in sight we joined this girl and after a few moments somebody came out of the nearby cabmen's shelter and seeing three women together started to talk to us in a bantering way. All this ended in our landing up with Joseph Ambridge, said to be the oldest night driver in Town, a little man with a greasy cap, and raincoat so worn that it had turned green. He had the eyes of a night-fighter and for thirty-six years had cruised through the streets of London between dusk and dawn. On one of the walls of the shelter hung a framed letter from Sir Ernest Shackleton, the explorer, thanking his cabmen friends for two pipes they gave him before he left for his final adventure. Ambridge said he had never stopped driving at night even during the raids, and had met with nothing worse than a few bruises when he drove over a time-bomb, but the shelter itself stood by a miracle. Its timber had been split when a very heavy bomb fell on a neighbouring hotel, hurling a great water tank across the road which upset thousands of gallons of water on the green shelter, turning it into a Noah's Ark.

CHRISTMAS was in the air. People were doing their last-minute shopping and the biggest queues were at the book-sellers' because, though publishers were rationed for paper, the public was able to buy all the volumes available without the vexation of coupons. This rush for literature of every description was one of the most striking features of the season. At some shops the scramble for best-sellers was so great that the last copies were taken from the windows, where they had been displayed to catch the attention of the passer-by. The book was the king of presents. It replaced so many of the things one could not obtain at any price. At Fortnum and Mason a beautifully painted notice announced: 'No whisky, no rum, no gin.' But the shop was crowded. There was nothing seasonal about the weather for on Christmas Eve the sun was almost as hot as in June. The main shopping arteries emptied as if by magic during the morning, leaving depleted stocks and harassed assistants.

I bought a small tree for the child. It stood without roots in a pot and the needles were already beginning to fall. My husband was at home and we decorated the tree with a few odds and ends, and gave a small tea party in Bobby's honour before taking him to a pantomime at the Stoll. A cab driver consented to take us on the condition we paid him double fare and it soon struck me that we had made a good bargain, for all up Piccadilly we drove past people frantically waving their arms and shouting themselves hoarse.

At the theatre the child leaned over the side of the box puzzling things out, but before the end of the first act he became restless and said he was hungry, and we decided to walk to the Savoy for something to eat. I crossed the foyer of the theatre holding the child by the hand and plunged into the dark night. As soon as he was in the street he began to chatter, but it was the blackout that aroused his interest, not the pantomime. This walk from Kingsway to the Strand, with a deep red moon like a ball of flame behind the Law Courts, enchanted his imagination, and was far more romantic than anything he had seen on the stage. He asked me a dozen questions, refused to admit it was cold though the wind had now become bitter, and I could feel his whole person trembling with the excitement of discovery, for it was the first time he had been out at night. I knew that I was holding a little Londoner by the hand—a tender being who already loved the roar of the fast car, the light from dimmed head-lamp, the shadows on the giant steel buildings, the mystery of the street. The meal was gay and we drank a bottle of champagne, but the room was by no means full. An American officer was supping alone at an adjoining table. He was obviously thinking of the family he had left behind and his eyes never left the blond child who was too young to realize the trials of separation. The waitress who served us was a refugee. She also was thinking of those whom she had left behind.

As soon as we returned home we put the child to bed and walked across Green Park and St James's to attend the midnight celebration of Holy Communion at Westminster Abbey. The town was deserted. St James's Park had an ethereal beauty that prepared one strangely for the service in honour of which no bells pealed. The moon covered the lake with a pale shroud, and a few water-birds floated against the reeds, their heads curled snugly beneath their wings. The stillness was broken only by Big Ben chiming the third quarter. One felt alone with one's Maker in the heart of the greatest city in the world.

1943

1943

OFTEN accompanied by Anne, the Angel of Brittany, I continued to wheel the child with the pekinese on his lap through the streets of an ever-changing London in war time. I felt no shame at all in doing no active war work or so blatantly pursuing my existence in a sort of privileged area whence so many young mothers with babies had fled. Conversely I was in such a state of elation that I never knew a moment of fear. What happened at the moment was ecstatically interesting. One never truly counted on being alive the next day.

New Year's morning found our village awakening after a night of revelry. The streets were hardly light and a lamp burned in Andrey's shop revealing the little Swiss-born newsagent, without collar or tie, bending over the newspapers laid out on his counter while the big black cat blinked on a bundle of magazines. The doors of Oscar's public house—the Shepherd—were wide open, allowing a draught to blow through the panelled bar, and charwomen were scrubbing the floor which had been trampled on by merrymakers the previous evening. The postman wished the greengrocer a happy New Year. An empty port bottle lay on the pavement outside the oil shop, mute witness of an orgy in the black-out.

From his pedestal in front of the India Office, Robert Clive peered across St James's Park. He carried a stick in his left hand and looked as if he were on the point of crossing the carriageway and calling in at Duck Island Cottage, home of Tom Hinton, the birdman.

This was an obvious place for Anne and me to bring the baby and the pekinese who sat together on the low-wheeled pram. Duck Island Cottage is much older than Robert Clive, whose birth in 1725 Anne discovered by consulting the notice on the pedestal. It was a low rambling house, or rather two lodges connected by a covered passage supported by stout tree trunks and roofed over with Virginia creeper which, on this first day of January, bereft of foliage, gave an appearance of thatching. Mrs Tom Hinton who lived here used to invite the child to watch her husband feeding the pelicans. She said, upon being wished a happy New Year, that her husband had gone over to the old boathouse and that she would take off her apron and go and fetch him, but she had hardly finished speaking before there were footsteps on the gravel and the birdman, wearing a worn raincoat and a bowler hat, appeared on the scene.

He was a man of over sixty, with a moustache changing colour at the ends. His voice was mellow and friendly. He asked Anne if she would like to see what a bomb had done to one of the houses in May 1941 and he took us round to where the privet hedge divided the garden from the reeds leading down to the waters of the lake. The bomb had done quite a lot of damage. At about 11 p.m. when he and his wife were crouching in the Anderson shelter, a heavy bomb dropped in the lake, drowning the little house in a gigantic waterspout. The chimney crashed through the tiles and the window panes were later replaced with the same composition of black tar as in my own apartment. As soon as day broke the birdman went round his island. He found a Garganey teal flung by the explosion into the topmost branch of an ash. A pelican lay dead on the rock where it was accustomed to sleep. There had been much slaughter amongst the birds, and those which survived were so nervous that they would not even come for their food. Only two pelicans were left on the island. One came from the United States and the other from Europe. Patiently, for the child's amusement, the birdman pointed out his rarer specimens—the Paradise shelduck from New Zealand, the Indian Ruddy shelduck with its golden head, and the blue-winged Abyssinian goose. Beyond the reeds where the ice was broken glided majestically a pair of magnificent swans born somewhere between Richmond and Windsor.

It must have been very pleasant to have, like Mr and Mrs Hinton, an island all of their own. It is the nearest thing to being a Robinson Crusoe. He had a rowing-boat in which he explored the coves and sought adventure round the rocks where the pelicans stood and flapped their wings. Thus my baby, like Peter Pan, rowed by the birdman in his little boat, found fairies in the heart of London in war time.

But we also knew the squire of Hyde Park, for just as Tom Hinton and his wife lived in St James's Park, Mr Duncan Campbell lived in Hyde Park. To all intents and purposes this Scotsman's house was his castle and Hyde Park his private estate, for after closing time, with the exception of the police station next door, Mr Campbell had the park to himself.

The railings had been removed so that some people might have contended that the Park was always open, but it closed officially, as it always did, at midnight, just as Kensington Gardens continued to close at dusk. Officials in Kensington Gardens went round calling out in stentorian voices, 'All out!', and they solemnly closed the big iron gates in spite of the fact that there were no railings.

Mr Campbell was the horticultural king of the central parks. He was the laird, if you prefer it, of Hyde Park, Kensington Gardens, St James's Park and the Green Park. He knew every plant and every tree, every hawthorn and every camomile lawn, and where the mushrooms were to be found on dew-stained mornings. He knew each mound and each hillock and where each bomb dropped. He knew where the daffodils and snowdrops slumbered under the hard winter ground. He had three or four acres of greenhouses, and it was he who decided each summer how to enliven the flowerbeds opposite Buckingham Palace. A short, stocky man, just turned sixty, he was once head gardener at Lord Islington's Wiltshire estate. You could not stump him in the name of a flower, a shrub, a tree or anything that grows in our fertile soil. He lived in half a pleasant red-brick house between the Serpentine and Marble Arch. The other half of the house was blown away in a night raid, but as soon as Mr Campbell went to live there he gathered up the pieces from the wreckage and built a sunken garden, with orange blossom growing all round.

'It is curious,' he said, 'but here is a point that may interest you two ladies. I found no evidence of a single sparrow being killed during the raids. Trees were uprooted, branches wrenched off, but our London sparrows seemed to have charmed lives.'

Thanks to the interest my baby invariably produced on Londoners going about their business during these war years, we invariably received smiling good-mornings from a very good-looking police inspector who plotted the various bombs that fell in Hyde Park. He had tried to count the incendiaries but after reaching the number 2,844 gave it up. Nevertheless coloured pennants on a huge map in his office showed the spot on which every known bomb fell during the air raids. On another map were marked the places where crimes had been committed during the past year. A murder headed the list—and the motive was love. There was also drama in another form. Picture a moonlit night with a pale glow shining phosphorescently on the cold waters of the Serpentine. A young man leaned over the west bridge, looking eastwards to where gleamed in the distance an almost Tartar collection of spires and domes. What thoughts ran through his brain that he should have so feverishly clambered over the parapet and plunged into the lake? 'What they don't know', said the inspector, 'is that the water here is shallower than anywhere else, so that these

would-be suicides generally land up with their feet stuck
in the mud and water below their shoulders.'

'Do you know where the ducks sleep at night?' he once
asked me. 'They sleep in the tops of the trees that skirt the
Serpentine, and that is where they build their nests. I have
seen mother ducks in the morning flopping down from the
boughs with their little ones on their back. Then they
waddle off into the water.'

About tramps he said: 'They work at night and sleep by
day. They go round London poking into refuse bins, and
each is a specialist. One collects old silk, another collects
leather, and yet another cigarette ends. They sleep on the
grass because of a paragraph in my book which says that
it is an offence to sleep on a bench.'

WHEN spring came, bringing warmer weather, I would sit
with a small group of women friends in what we called the
Green Park drawing-room, and while we talked and knitted,
Bobby and the pekinese could play safely on the grass under
the shadow of the Ritz and Arlington House. Towards tea
time I would take the child and the little dog back to the
apartment where they would remain happily by themselves
while I went shopping. Often I returned to find Margaret
giving Bobby his bath. Margaret worked as a maid in
Carrington House, but with a dignity all of her own and an
affection for my son which made her come whenever possible to take him for a walk or to help with his bedtime
preparations.

Margaret had been in service all her life. Her voice was
refined and slightly plaintive. She had been accustomed to
families with all the hierarchy of the backstairs: cook, lady's
maid, parlour maids, butler, coachman and the rest. She
had served in homes where the master or the mistress held
morning prayers in the drawing-room, and she claimed that
this provided a welcome rest while the servants looked out
at the ancestral trees in the park. I asked her whether, if she

were young again, she would prefer the old days or the
modern idea of a small flat, the radio and a night off each
week, but she was non-committal. From time to time she
took Bobby on shopping expeditions, during which she
prudently invested her money in pots and pans or wool or
china, which she expected would increase in value, and she
was surprisingly successful.

Margaret had a room on the first floor with central
heating and a bathroom. Her room was filled with treasures
that Bobby loved to examine. She had a habit of humming
church music which my child absorbed and gave voice to
next day. He had the utmost faith in her, even when she
limited his bath-water because of the war. I often wondered
what connection there could be in his mind between the
hot-water tap and the drone of the distant bomber.

HAVING lunched in Soho my friend Paloma and I walked
home through Berwick Market. Summer had come and a
coster's barrow filled with cherries was drawn up by the
kerb in Pulteney Street. About fifty women had formed
themselves into a queue in front of the barrow while the
coster was quietly finishing his meal in the local public-
house. To appreciate what was strange about this scene, I
must point out that at this time there was a great rush for
what the Ministry of Food called 'soft fruit'. We had been
told that in a few days' time all the strawberries, cherries
and gooseberries would be made into jam, and as soon as
this happened we would have to go without dessert. Every
London housewife, therefore, wanted to remind herself
what a strawberry, a cherry or a gooseberry looked like
before these luscious gifts of summer were spirited away,
but unfortunately there were not nearly sufficient to go
round. What a revolution was caused by the sight of an
unattended barrow filled to the brim with ripe red cherries!
In any other country, housewives, who become furies on
such occasions, would have set about the barrow and served

themselves. But here in the heart of London, fifty women, hungry for cherries, were calmly waiting for the coster to finish his cheese and beer, and, what is more, in order to preserve a sense of justice, they had queued up. Meanwhile the coster himself, under no illusion about the value of the treasure he had left unguarded in the street to tempt passers-by, was so sure of the Londoners' honesty that he did not even hurry to finish his meal. During early spring when daffodils sold at half a guinea a dozen in the shops, the lawns of our London parks were golden with them and nobody ever thought of stealing a bunch at night, though the absence of railings made them readily accessible. There were tulips and hyacinths also that would have made any burglar rich. Yet not a single one was ever picked.

A little farther along we came on a shop which sold all manner of stationery, and in the window Paloma noticed a collection of water-colours which she wished to buy for Bobby. We went in to ask for some cobalt blue, but the assistant shook his head sadly and answered: 'They are all dummies.' 'Ah,' said I. 'Well, may I have a red pencil?' 'I am sorry, Madam, no more coloured pencils.' 'Then show me a fountain pen.' 'A fountain pen, Madam, we haven't even got a steel nib.' 'Then what have you got?' I asked. The assistant smiled sympathetically. 'Heaven knows!' he answered. From Pulteney Street we continued our way through Golden Square into Regent Street to call at Jaeger's, where I hoped to discover a few ounces of knitting wool, but there had not been any wool since early December and none was expected. By now it had started to rain, and we waited a few moments by Fuller's cake counter, in front of which a women wearing a Tyrolese blouse, heartened by the sudden influx of shoppers, paced up and down shaking a collection box and crying out: 'Don't forget the lifeboat men—twenty-six lives saved every week.' Having collected all the pennies forthcoming from our little crowd, she continued to keep up her mono-logue interspersed with remarks on the weather and other topics of interest, so that we left her with these words still ringing in our ears: 'Don't forget the lifeboat men—I wonder if it's going to rain all the afternoon?—Twenty-six lives saved every day—My dear, have you noticed that with all this talk about the shortage of leather, the shoe shop next door has closed for a week?—Don't forget the lifeboat men—Oh, thank you, madam. Every little counts.'

The rain had stopped as suddenly as it had fallen, and a mid-June sun was already drying the pavements.

I was fortunate in the friends I made in our Green Park drawing-room. With the exception of Anne and one or two other girls, most of the women were older and much more experienced in the real, deep problems of life than I was, and looking back I find myself immensely grateful for what they taught me and the innumerable kindnesses they showed me. My mother whom we had left behind on the quay at St Malo was constantly in my thoughts, and the fact that I had been willing to leave her there alone, without money, gave me constant nightmares. My own health which had never been strong was just then beginning to show the strain of all the anxieties and worries that followed my flight from France and my attempt to guard the child through all the dangers of a city at war. My mother-in-law who lived in Surrey was much too old to start projecting herself into my various dilemmas and I was far too proud ever to ask for help, either morally or financially. The dozen or so women of several nationalities, some English, some French, some Belgian, who had all lived in London most of their lives, taught me that friendships between women can be something immensely rewarding and precious. Not only did they help form my character at this time but all in different ways came to my help (as I went to theirs) when anything went desperately wrong.

Those of us who met almost every afternoon in this open-air drawing-room were watched over by a little man with sallow cheeks. On most days he wore a neat brown suit, and over his right shoulder was slung a machine with which to punch tickets. His job was to wander round and round the Green Park collecting coppers from the people who sat on the hard green chairs or the more comfortable deck-chairs. Our so-called drawing-room was located on an L-shaped lawn overlooking Piccadilly. It was a pleasant green stretch bordered by coils of barbed wire (which had been placed there for some reason that nobody was ever able to fathom), a high wicker fence, on the other side of which were the trenches that had not been used since they were first frantically dug during the Munich crisis, and a large sump on which each spring appeared a couple of ducks which wanted to form a family away from the feathered congestion of the lake in St James's Park.

The little man with the sallow cheeks arrived on the lawn just after eleven o'clock every morning and his first care was to review the chairs to see that they were drawn up in twos at frequent intervals on the grass. Every day he placed the broken deck-chairs against a tree trunk. Business was not very brisk before lunch, and he would have time to search the lawn for any of the things that people were apt to leave behind, and sometimes he would stand for a few moments to watch American soldiers practising baseball on the strip of grass on the other side of the gravel alley. That little section of the Green Park had become American territory by right of conquest, and we would no more have thought of intruding than the doughboys would have tried to play ball in the drawing-room.

The chair seller had the faintest trace of an accent which struck one of us as strange. She opened up a little cautious conversation starting with the weather, and leading on to more personal details—whether he was married and had any children, and what he had done before punching tickets in the Park.

His name was René Dijon, and he was one of the most famous pastrycooks in Europe. He had worked with such culinary giants as Escoffier and Mallet, and he could talk about the halcyon days of princes and the Café Royal in the early 1900s, when discerning Edwardians sent him congratulatory notes for his ethereal masterpieces which simply melted in the mouth. For thirty years he had practised his art at the Grand Hotel at Folkestone—until it was closed down at the beginning of the war. Now, contented in mind and satisfied with little, he was spending the evening of his life philosophically walking from chair to chair. His son was in the British Army and, having worked his way up from private to captain, was in Malta, from which heroic island he wrote that life had become almost dull since the raids had ended.

We used to ask him how to make cakes with dried eggs and margarine. Although the poor man had never made a cake with fewer than a dozen new-laid eggs and as much butter as was deemed necessary to satisfy the tastes of the most difficult potentates, he lived up to the reputation that good workmen make the best of what they have in hand, and he gave his first lesson with admirable patience. In the afternoon his client returned with a sample of her handiwork, and this Mr Dijon tasted under the spreading branches of an elm tree.

SATURDAY 10th July 1943 will pass into history as the day when the Allied forces invaded Sicily, thus establishing the second front in Europe so eagerly awaited by the civilized world. The news was not received in time for it to be printed in the morning papers, which devoted much of their space to a question that, though of less urgency, was near to the heart of Londoners. The question was nothing less than the replanning of the capital city over a long period, possibly over half a century.

There were proposals for new roads, bridges and open spaces, an embankment for the south side of the Thames, and a new treatment of Westminster providing what the

The Green Park drawing-room

Shepherd Market: a London Bobby

Shepherd Market: Andrey's shop

The magic city

This is Piccadilly Circus, son

Coventry Street

authors called a really permanent atmosphere of dignity and calm.

Quite clearly London would have to be remodelled after the war. Her scars were deeper than some of us realized. Vast areas had been mown down as with a scythe. Entire streets would have to be rebuilt. Behind façades which still kept up an air of normality were pits of desolation in which nettles grew. The building boom after the 1914–18 war would be as nothing compared to what would take place after this one, and if anything was certain it was that London would not be rebuilt as we had known it in pre-war days. A nobler city might well rise on the ruins of the one that had grown up haphazardly over centuries, but it was not without sorrow that many of us resigned ourselves to the fact that in our old age we should find hardly any trace of the London of our youth. For the time being we lived in a Town of betwixt and between. Let us consider the City for example. We could close our eyes and remember vaguely what certain parts of it looked like two years ago. We opened our eyes and were confronted with wide vistas looking something like Pompeii with a lot of cellar walls and a few gutted churches. The horror of the flames had disappeared. In Gresham Street, at the corner of Foster Lane, I came across the most beautiful garden arranged on what a few months earlier had been mere rubble. It was known in the district as 'The Garden of Paradise' and was tended by the verger of the adjoining and ruined St Anne and St Agnes with St John Zachary. There were hollyhocks and evening primroses. There were little paths and rockeries and a few people were basking in the sunshine in deckchairs. On a low wall was this plaque, all that remained of the former church: 'On this site stood St John Zachary, destroyed in the Great Fire of 1666.' The building on which the City Corporation had fixed this memorial tablet was, in turn, burned to the ground in the Great Fire of 1940. Devastation stretched ahead as far as the eye could reach, but here and there were famous churches—St Alban, Wood

Street, on the left, and St Mary the Virgin, Aldermanbury, with its bust of Shakespeare still standing in the churchyard, to the right; and far in the distance rose the stark walls of St Giles', Cripplegate.

Somebody was laying down a grass lawn in the vicinity of Paternoster Row, which historic street our children would never know. A future Dickens would have to describe for their benefit the dark alleyways and grimy warehouses that smelt of printer's ink and paper. Wide boulevards would probably be carved across these ghost-ridden sites, but not till after the war, so that now, even if we had a little difficulty in remembering exactly where buildings and streets stood and what they looked like, our memories were not jarred by new planning. A house or a church or even half a street shaded by an age-old poplar spared by the enemy's fire bombs helped us to reconstruct in our mind what had gone. We had thus one eye on the past and the other on the future. We were able to cling to our old loves, knowing that this state of things would not be for long, for when the new City took shape, it would not only rise above the empty spaces but would also hew down any modest piece of old London that got in its way. Who in these busy days would recall with adequate affection those parts of our Town that were bound to be swept away?

That evening, having left Bobby in the charge of Margaret, I was passing through St James's Park on the way to meet my husband at the Ministry of Production when I came upon Mr C. J. Purnell, the secretary of the London Library. The one hundred and second annual meeting of this institution in St James's Square had just revealed that the membership was larger than it had ever been and that the financial report was the best in a quarter of a century. This news was not altogether surprising, for the revival of reading throughout the country was common knowledge, and perhaps the most interesting development was the wide call for serious literature. Mr Purnell was proving himself a worthy successor to Hagberg Wright. During the great raids on London, while his son was distinguishing himself in the R.A.F., he had watched over the library unceasingly, and still continued to sleep in the basement with the fire-watchers. He was never far from his precious volumes but strolled every morning and every evening through St James's Park.

He was sitting on a bench opposite Duck Island and we walked round the lake together. The Park was really looking at its best. The mulberries were ripening and the fig trees on either side of the suspension bridge filled the evening air with their pungent perfume. On various occasions when as the woman guest I lunched with friends in the City I had been interested in the thick clusters of tall plants with rose-tinted blooms and long pointed leaves that everywhere covered the worst scars of the bombed sites. An aquatic variety of these plants was to be seen along the fringe of the lake and I asked Mr Purnell if he could tell me its name. I found him well able to answer my question, because he had recently attended a remarkable lecture by Professor E. J. Salisbury on 'The Flora of Bombed Areas' at the Royal Institution, in the course of which the Professor had made particular reference to this plant, known as the rosebay willowherb. Somebody recorded after the Great Fire of London in 1666 that the ruins round St Paul's were covered by the London rocket, but a century and a half later this plant had become extremely rare and Professor Salisbury failed to find a single specimen. On the other hand, the rosebay willowherb flourished on nearly ninety per cent of the bombed sites which the Professor examined. The interesting thing about this discovery was that the rosebay willowherb attracted the attention of botanists before the war because of its particular affection for burnt heaths, which had become more frequent since the cigarette and the motor car. It was therefore already associated with areas devastated by fire. The rosebay uses a parachute to disseminate its seed-pods. Thus in the same way that devastation came to our fair city from the air, so did Nature cover the scars by aerial propagation.

The Professor discovered that a close runner-up to the rosebay willowherb was the Oxford ragwort which came from Sicily on whose soil our soldiers were that day landing! The ragwort liked the volcanic ashes round Mount Etna and found a sympathetic terrain in our burnt-out London buildings. It first came to Britain in 1794, where it was seen growing on walls in and around Oxford.

Mr Purnell was much better informed than I was about the wild-fowl on the lake. His knowledge seemed almost to rival that of Mr Hinton, the birdman. He showed me the nests of the coots, whose young wear red hats which turn to white as they grow older. We watched the diving ducks and the Abyssinian geese, and when I asked him how he learned all the species by name he said he took a good note of any bird that seemed strange to him and then looked it up at the library on his return. The lime trees were in flower, and their scent was so strong that people who passed under them stopped in surprise to glance up into the foliage.

A tall distinguished man with white hair passed us and greeted my companion. 'That is Admiral X,' said Mr Purnell. 'During the raids he and his wife were generally the last to leave the library. They live close by. One night the Admiral went out for a stroll. When he returned he found that his home had been hit and his wife was dead.'

A week before the August Bank Holiday the crowds at the big London termini were so large that thousands of people, unable to find any room on the long-distance expresses, spent the night on the platforms waiting for morning. Factory workers were determined to have a change. Those who worked in London wanted to go to the country; those who worked in the country wished to come to Town. All felt they had worked well during the long months and now deserved some recompense. They were ready for any hardships their holiday entailed—ready even to sleep on the beach between coils of barbed wire. Victories were being won with the arms they had forged. The fortunes of war had changed in our favour. Three years ago we were waiting for the enemy to invade our shores. Today three-quarters of Sicily was in our hands, and as our war workers started their holiday the Italian people suffered the anguish they had hoped to impose on us. Mussolini was preparing to throw in the sponge. Tears replaced the laughter of our adversaries.

As London became fuller, as fresh waves of American troops reached the capital and young men fleeing from bondage arrived from the occupied countries of Europe, Piccadilly from the Green Park to the Circus, and Coventry Street, from the Circus to Leicester Square, became increasingly animated and picturesque.

This straight line, little more than half a mile long, became Allied Main Street. It was not only the favourite beat of the Londoner. War workers from the provinces thronged the pavements seeking glamour. Troops from the Empire and Americans from the forty-eight States described it in letters home. Thousands of them would keep to the end of their days memories of this—the most famous half-mile on the face of the globe. Some who arrived on leave did not know a soul in Town. They were drawn here as if by a magnet, and their hours of liberty, between trains, were spent swelling the crowds, queueing up for cinemas, striking chance friendships in the bars or fun-fairs. They felt less lonely where the crowds were most dense.

Sometimes we used to join the procession on Sunday afternoons towards five o'clock, when Shepherd Market was half asleep and when Andrey, the newsagent, could be seen locking up his shop before going to the pictures. The Green Park had a crowd that had nothing in common with the weekday habitués. They were country cousins and folks from the outer perimeter. Traffic in Piccadilly was so light that a green dray-cart filled with American soldiers and their girl friends and drawn by two white shire horses clattered at full speed past Hatchard's. The driver's whip was garlanded and everybody was singing 'Idaho', the melancholy strains of which were wafted away in the breeze. A notice outside St James's, Piccadilly, announced an open-air service in the churchyard for 6.30, and a middle-aged woman with a blue hat was putting out chairs on the cracked flagstones between which grew sturdy rosebay.

Crowds poured into the Piccadilly Hotel, where an Italian maître d'hôtel who never talked politics and who had been there during the war of 1914–18 showed them into the already packed *thé dansant*. Just inside Eagle Place, the short alley leading from Piccadilly to Jermyn Street, the famous tramp with the long unkempt beard and the limp brown hat, not pinched at the crown but domed like a sugar-loaf, was fast asleep beside his limited collection of second-hand Victorian novelettes. Two itinerant vendors were selling their wares displayed on the sandbags next to the Monseigneur—one was selling tinted spectacles, the other roses made up into buttonholes. A tall London bobby, wearing the peacetime helmet that by now had replaced the tin hat of two years earlier, was looking imperturbably at the various military police parading in twos round the Circus—American, French, Dutch—and two girl soldiers with red caps and 'M.P.' on their armlets.

Coventry Street was more crowded than Piccadilly. The slow-moving waves outside Lyons Corner House surged round the two entrances, and against the long queue of patient folk waiting for permission to enter the tea-room situated at the far end of the dim foyer. Another queue had formed for the 1s 4d cafeteria. There was yet another in Rupert Street opposite the Prince of Wales Theatre, but this one had nothing to do with either the Corner House or the theatre. People were waiting to buy cherries from a stall in the middle of the street. There were similar scenes all along the route, queues for plums, for apples, and even for peaches. Everything interested the crowds. They stood in contemplation in front of Keith Prowse reading the titles of the popular music-hall scores: 'I see you everywhere', 'Some day we shall meet again', 'By the light of the silvery moon', 'Taking a chance on love', 'A fool with a dream.'

The Rialto, one of the West End's oldest picture-houses, was giving its last performance of *We Dive at Dawn*. The shored-up entrance to the Café de Paris bore a notice saying: 'Danger—Unsafe Premises.' Etam, where I used to buy my silk stockings and take them to be mended, announced that it was closed for stocktaking. In common with other women in London it was to be another year before I wore my first nylons brought in my case as a tremendous gift from America.

In the middle of the road an Australian flying officer was limping along on crutches. Three girls wearing white linen skirts shot past him on bicycles, but were brought to a stop by the traffic lights. Two policewomen were looking at a print dress displayed in one of the windows of Stagg and Russell. One said to the other: 'It's lovely, isn't it? Do you think it would suit me, dear?' Her natural femininity was touching and made me feel as sad and hungry for nice things as she was.

On the other side of the road the Automobile Association building seemed strangely silent but full of memories of the carefree days when one toured the country in a two-seater car. The A.A. realized this, for in one of its windows was displayed a picture of a country road in peace time—lines of family cars being given the friendly salute by an A.A. scout. Over the picture one read, 'Until these days return!' The reference was to two pictures, on either side of which showed the same country road filled with military traffic. In the next window we saw two Tommies in the turret of a tank in the Libyan desert looking back at an A.A. scout disappearing in a cloud of sand. One Tommy was saying to the other, 'Trouble ahead, Bert. He didn't salute.' Past these harmless little jokes surged the slowly trudging crowds eager to laugh at anything. They overflowed into every establishment open on Sunday afternoon. They refreshed themselves at a milk bar between Dolcis and the Ritz Cinema, where *Gone with the Wind* had been running for four years. Our milk bars remind the Americans of their ice-cream parlours. This one had yellow walls and silver fans hanging from the ceiling. It sold frozen apple pie and what it called Delikrema, ice-cream sodas, parfaits and milk shakes. Its patrons sat on high stools or congregated in groups (I have seen the sailors of five nations gesticulating together), while on the pavement the long queue waited to enter the Empire, where Joan Crawford was playing in *Above Suspicion*.

On either side of the Monseigneur News Cinema, whose main attraction consisted of pictures from Sicily, were the Queen's Brasserie and the Queen's Bar. In Leicester Place, which leads into Lisle Street, two employees of the N.S.P.C.C. were sitting on kitchen chairs on the doorstep and one of them was meditatively munching a sandwich, while the society's black cat purred on his lap. One sensed here the foreign influence of nearby Soho, for a little farther along the street was a restaurant with two tables in the open air like in continental cities. The tables had Basque cloths and stood on a carpet of synthetic grass. An R.A.F officer and a girl were sitting at one of them eating spam and drinking Algerian wine.

Some of the crowd surged on past the Café de l'Europe and Warner's as far as the Hippodrome, which enjoyed success after success since the beginning of the war. George Black was producing *Lisbon Story* and outside the theatre were photographs of the cast. The Hippodrome marked the end of the half-mile, and though some people wandered into Charing Cross Road, most retraced their steps into Leicester Square. Warner's was showing *Mission to Moscow*, a film made from the book by the U.S. Ambassador Davis. Two or three people stood on the kerb offering the book for sale; others pushed pamphlets in front of passers-by as they cried out: '*Mission to Moscow* falsifies history—read the tract, price one penny.'

On my way back I cut across the square where Shake-speare stood in the middle of the gardens, a pigeon perched on his head. There was shade in the gardens from the four big trees round the playwright and colour from the light-blue flowers planted at his feet. Some of the trees on the outer perimeter were destroyed in the raids. These were replaced by young trees to give shade to future generations. Many people sought the cool of the gardens. They rested on the benches. An R.A.F. mechanic and his girl-friend were reading the same book held up jointly. A sailor was fast asleep. An American soldier was sitting on a pedestal which had once served for a bust of Reynolds, but Reynolds was destroyed in an air raid. The biggest crowds gazed eastwards towards the ebony tower of the Odeon—the monster cinema which stands on the site of the Alhambra, where the Bing Boys played to crowded houses in the 1914–18 war. The Café Anglais carried on business in what used to be its foyer, turned into a bar. The old restaurant that enjoyed a boom during the first six months of the war— the phoney war—was a yard opened by high explosives to the sky and beer-barrels stood on the erstwhile dance-floor. Geraniums decorated the front of the Café Anglais and made a blaze of colour.

It was past eight o'clock and the scene along the half-mile was beginning to change. The pay-boxes of the cinemas were closed and the commissionaire of the Rialto stood on a ladder changing the title of the big film. *The Life and Death of Colonel Blimp* would tomorrow take the place of *We Dive at Dawn* and the commissionaire was spelling out the words to himself as he changed the letters. The metal hands of the game of chance at the Sports Palace were still hovering over packets of playing-cards and boxes of matches; the itinerant vendors were packing up their barrows from which mountains of cherries and plums had disappeared; the queue for tea at the Corner House had gone, and in its place there was another for supper. The man in the foyer was crying out: 'There's room on the second floor . . . no waiting on the second floor.' A group of Americans standing in the centre of Coventry Street shouted lustily for a taxi.

From Shaftesbury Avenue came a tall policeman riding a very small bicycle. He carried over his shoulder a long rod that looked like a pike, and when he reached the first traffic lights of the Circus he jumped off his machine and with the help of the rod lowered the half-shutters that must dim the traffic lights before the blackout. This routine became necessary when it was decided a short time earlier to increase the amount of green, amber, and red during the daytime. Motorists complained that they could not see the lights clearly. So the lowering of the shutters had become a London scene every evening. The police cycled round with their rods like the lamp-lighters of our youth. Only they dimmed the lights instead of putting them on. It would seem to be a case of progress in reverse.

CHARLIE the milkman was still doing his rounds. In my constant effort to obtain milk and eggs I used occasionally to chase our milkman or one of his colleagues as far as Soho, and these frantic expeditions, over and above all my other commitments, often exhausted me. It was not that the rations were in themselves inadequate, but when one has a child of four milk is the basis of so many things, and my chief business in life was clearly to keep him healthy. Lack of proper food during the war of 1914-18 was the cause of my own health remaining poor ever since. Any mother who had suffered as much as I had from under-nourishment when she was little would have been as nervous for her offspring as I was during a second war.

Accordingly I used to go from street to street in search of Charlie and the little horse which drew the milk float. As there was so little traffic I could often hear the tinkling of the milk bottles a quarter of a mile away and then, like a squaw, I would follow the sound. At other times Charlie would leave the little horse and the milk float and descend area steps or conversely climb to the top of rickety buildings, putting out milk bottles at every floor, occasionally being invited by some woman into her kitchen for a cigarette and a cup of tea. As Margaret was not always available to look after Bobby, I would leave him alone in the apartment with the pekinese. I never feared for their safety. Everybody knew them. All the neighbours would protect them. London in war time was extraordinarily honest. What with this constant running after Charlie and the daily queueing up for almost everything I caught a succession of chills that prepared the way for a grave inflammation of the sinus. For weeks on end I was never without the most excruciating headaches, and tears flowed from my swollen eyes but I was so afraid to check the momentum of my daily routine that I increasingly doped myself with aspirin. When finally I consulted a famous Harley Street specialist he decided to pierce the cartilage of my nose and introduce a drain without even a local anaesthetic. There were, of course, no antibiotics, no penicillin, at least for unimportant civilians, and I have seldom suffered a worse torture. Even the forceps were hardly more painful. I left Harley Street on a moonless night in the blackout, my head swathed in a shawl. Short-sighted I stumbled over sandbags, hit myself against railings, searched desperately for a passing taxi. Nevertheless, though I was obliged to walk all the way home, I had a marvellous night, dreaming I was cured. With morning, the pain returned twofold and I was obliged to go back to my specialist, who on this occasion consented to administer sufficient gas to keep me unconscious for a part, at any rate, of a second operation.

I dreamt the most beautiful dream. I was in an orchard full of apple blossom and as I looked up entranced the blossom began to fall over me until my hair was covered in pink petals. Then the gas gave out and to my horror the work had hardly begun!

The tragedies that give way to feminine depression appear

trifling in the telling. On my return to the apartment Crouch, the head porter, informed me that my laundry basket with nearly all the linen I possessed had disappeared, presumably stolen, and for some technical reason which appeared quite logical to him, I had absolutely no redress. The other women in the Green Park drawing-room all did their best to help me and Paloma gave me a sheet. 'Cut it in two,' she said, 'that will make you the pair!' On top of all this a different specialist told me that I had a patch on a lung and that if it was infected I would be separated from my child. For the best part of a week I tasted the abomination of despair. I could not even have dared go for the X-ray if I had not been taken there by another woman from our coterie, a woman of infinite understanding and experience. The examination proved negative as far as infection was concerned. Life began to flow normally again. I had a final, curious experience which only could have happened in the middle of a war. At tea time I used to listen to a serial on the B.B.C. called, I think, 'The Robinsons'. A baby whose parents had not wanted it to be vaccinated against diphtheria was in the gravest danger, and we were all waiting to hear if the doctors, in spite of the parents' fault, would succeed in saving its life. The next morning Bobby, as was his custom, was standing on a low stool in the living-room that allowed him to look out through the open window into the courtyard. A taxi came into the yard, deposited its customer and was about to drive off again when the taxi-driver changed his mind, left the driving seat and walked across to the child at the window where, looking at Bobby, he said to me: 'I hope you've had the little boy vaccinated against diphtheria. Remember what happened to the Robinson baby!'

Yes, London was an incredible city!

THE Summer Exhibition at the Royal Academy showed a marked reaction away from the orgy of shelter scenes, bombed houses, rest centres, and such harrowing subjects as ships sinking in the middle of the ocean, which had been so prominent before. David Jagger exhibited a portrait of Lady Bedingfeld and another of Lady Inchcape, and both women wore evening gowns! Augustus John had given an exhibition of drawings at the Leicester Galleries which was his first for several years. Both men and women visitors put on John costume, in incredibly bright colours, in honour of the artist's love for gypsy colouring. John himself wore a green corduroy suit with a voluminous light beige overcoat.

Lord Methuen, a staff captain in the Scots Guards, gave an exhibition of London landscapes featuring Wren buildings. One of the pictures—shown not at the Leicester Galleries but at Burlington House, I think—had been painted during the Battle of London. He had set up his easel on the roof of a tall building in Whitehall and every night left the canvas under a tarpaulin. The building was hit but the canvas was undamaged.

For about a fortnight, almost as soon as it was dark, many of our bombers on their way to targets in Germany flew right over Piccadilly. The grim procession often took nearly an hour to pass over, and during this time it was almost impossible to think of anything else. The continual drone of the motors hummed in our ears, and it seemed that destiny was grinding out slow vengeance upon the enemy who not so very long ago had sought to wipe out London with its air armada. Many hurried into the streets to look up at the navigation lights of our bombers, and from time to time one or other of the machines would flash the victory sign. We wondered where these boys were going—to Berlin, to Munich, or the Rhine? Some of them might not come back. Their machines would be attacked by German night fighters while we slept safely in our beds. We had not heard so many bombers since the enemy flew over London in the opposite direction taking destruction to our great industrial cities of the Midlands. Thus it had been when Coventry was attacked.

On Wednesday evening, 8th September, we learned of Italy's unconditional surrender. I telephoned Anne who gave a cry of joy, but almost immediately what was realist in her nature began to assess the immediate results of the great news on French patriots, who for so long now had been grimly wrestling against the invader. I knew that she was curbing her emotions, for her voice, after showing every sign of excitement, became quite steady as she said: 'This means that the patriots hiding in the mountains will be able to join the Allies by escaping into Italy. It's the opening of another door.' I am certain that for long after I rang off she must have remained as if in a dream, trying to figure out which of the mountain passes she would take if, instead of being safely in London, she was sharing the dangers and adventures of her sturdy compatriots.

My thoughts were disturbed by a ring from Charles, whose character was so different from that of Anne. He was quite delirious. 'I'm going right out into the streets', he exclaimed, 'to see the rejoicings, unless, of course, you Londoners take your victories as phlegmatically as you take your defeats. In that case I'll look up the Poles and the Dutch or even old Berlemont in Soho. I feel like a locomotive with steam up and I've simply got to let it out. Can you imagine what scenes there will be in Paris and in Brussels this evening?' 'Perhaps they won't know yet!' I answered. He laughed so heartily that I was obliged to hold the telephone receiver at arm's length so as not to be deafened. 'You don't know them,' he said; 'news travels even faster in the occupied countries than here. I wager my native city will be in a turmoil this evening. What would I not give to be there! I've just heard that my son's voice has broken. He says he speaks like a man now and looks forward to acting like one. I almost expect to run up against him in

Piccadilly one day, for if there is a chance to escape he will certainly take it.'

Poor Charles was almost drunk with joy and pride and he rang off abruptly to hurry into the streets.

Piccadilly was crowded just before dusk, but there was nothing unusual to reveal the satisfaction that people felt at the tremendous news. Many seemed to think with President Roosevelt: 'The time has not yet come for celebration, and I have a suspicion that when this war does end, we shall not be in a very celebrating frame of mind.'

WE HAD been to a cocktail party at the top of the building and the lift was bringing us down from the seventh floor.

A woman, with a mink coat and a little fur hat which was half hidden by her hair curled up in front of it, looked down at Bobby with eyes that seemed to laugh all by themselves. She was looking at him because he was still very small and there is something delightfully ingenuous in a child of his age, and also because of an insignia with a star on it which an American soldier had fastened to the arm of his new coat. She asked him who had given the star, and as soon as she spoke she betrayed the rich Southern drawl of the cotton plantations of Alabama.

Her name was Dorothy Berker and she worked in the Rainbow Club, the vast American Red Cross centre that overlooked the boxed-up statue of Eros in Piccadilly Circus.

The next day, at tea time, she brought to our flat two Americans from Chicago. These boys, Ralph Gault and Wayne Wolter, friends since childhood, had just been reunited on the floor of the Rainbow. One of them was in a Coastguard Flotilla. He had taken part in the invasion of Sicily. His friend was in the Ordnance Service. They were young and shy and unbelievably grateful for this fleeting glimpse of English family life.

Dorothy Berker was born in Montgomery, Alabama.

Her warm accent endeared her to the 'G.I.s,' as American soldiers called themselves now, for the term 'doughboy' had long since gone out. G.I. stands for Government Issue. The soldier of today receives all he needs from a thoughtful Government. Every day Mrs Berker must have told several hundred soldiers where she was born. It was the first question they asked her. 'Montgomery, Alabama,' she would say, 'and still a rebel. And when we finish off this war, we'll go back and get the other one over.' This introduction invariably produced a happy smile.

Mrs Berker was one of the first tenants in our monster building. She had lived there off and on since 1935 between journeys to New York, Paris and Cannes. The large windows of her flat overlooked the roofs of Mayfair. Her drawing-room was decorated in light shades, and amongst the books in her built-in shelves I found *Gone with the Wind*, which might just as well have been the story of Alabama as of Georgia. One of her forbears, during the Civil War, ran the blockade with satins and ostrich feathers for the southern belles, who wanted finery for their bonnets.

Dorothy Berker was caught in America at the outbreak of this war, having flown there in the Clipper towards the end of the summer. She had, in her own words, 'a heck of a time getting back', but in the spring of 1940 she sailed in the *Manhattan* to Naples.

We were still in the period of waiting and watching known as the 'phoney' war. Something warned Mrs Berker that she would never again see Europe as it was then. It was the twilight of the pre-war continent. Instead of hurrying to London, therefore, she dawdled on the way, spending a few weeks at Capri, visiting Rome, where Mr Sumner Welles, the American diplomat, had just arrived, and going on to Paris in time for Easter. April in Paris! There was a song of this name which swept two continents at the time of the Coronation. Never had the chestnut trees in the Champs-Elysées looked more lovely than during this spring, when France stood unsuspectingly on the brink of defeat.

The milk float

Whitehorse Street,
Piccadilly

Mrs Berker went to the races at Longchamps. By the time she reached London, the Germans had invaded Norway.

During the Battle of Britain, Mrs Berker made one more trip to America on business. During her spare time she helped to welcome British sailors in the United States. As soon as she could get back to England, she resolved to make Americans feel less lonely in London, for her countrymen were arriving here in ever-increasing numbers.

I had often passed the Rainbow in Shaftesbury Avenue and wondered what it was like inside. The Government had commandeered for it two famous London landmarks— the Monico and the adjoining Lyons; the American Red Cross had instilled the atmosphere of home. The pavement outside was always crowded with G.I.s, and as there was also a busy bus stop here, one generally had to fight one's way past. It all helped to make that effervescence that marked the heart of the Empire.

Mrs Berker suggested that I should spend a morning with her behind the long information counter in the foyer of the Rainbow to get an idea what interested the Americans during their leave in Town. I accepted her invitation one Saturday in mid November.

The hall was very full. There were sign-posts nailed to the pillars: 'Why lose your money, watch, or camera? Please check them here.' An arrow, pointing vaguely east towards Leicester Square, bore the inscription: 'Berlin— 600 miles.' Another, pointing in the direction of Regent Street, said: 'New York—3,271 miles.'

Mrs Berker's post was at the far end of the counter, along which there were about a dozen girls wearing grey overalls with blue epaulets, anxious to solve any problems that might come from the boys on the other side. I sat on a high stool between Dorothy Berker and Kay Peters, a London girl who was trying to forget the night when her father and mother were killed by a bomb which destroyed their little house at Elstree. 'I was taking cover in a cupboard,' said Kay. 'Father was just leaving to fire-watch in our street.

Mother had run after him. The rescue squad found father's legs on the doorstep. The roof fell on mother. She died in hospital.'

This work suited Kay, whose only chance to sleep at night was to return to her flat physically exhausted.

Mrs Berker had discovered half a dozen taxi-drivers who knew something about the history of London. These drivers reported to her at stated times of the day to collect American soldiers anxious to see Buckingham Palace, Westminster Abbey, Whitehall and St Paul's.

The drivers acted as guides. 'I find out what they know,' said Dorothy Berker, 'and then I give it back to them the way our boys will understand it.' The tour lasted a couple of hours and cost each soldier six shillings. One of these trips was due to start in a few minutes. Mrs Berker was trying to collect five strangers who would be friends by the time they were back. Five boys who would probably like each other, take tea together and then go to the movies.

'Hey, Butch,' she called across the counter, 'how'd you like to see Westminster Abbey and St Paul's? You sit in a taxi and all the sights roll past you.'

'O.K. When do we start?'

'In five minutes. What's your name, son?'

'Clapper.'

'Where do you come from, Clapper?'

'I'll give you three guesses.'

'I haven't time to play, honey.'

'New York, ma'am.'

'Where in New York?'

'Auburn.'

'Isn't that the place they've got a jail?'

'Sure. How do you know?'

The soldier was leaning over the counter and his eyes were fixed on Dorothy's bracelet. It was made of heavy gold signets that Victorian gentlemen used to wear suspended from their watch-chains. The seals rang against one another and clanged against the surface of the counter.

'Now,' he said, taking her wrist and catching gingerly hold of one of the signets, 'tell me about your jewellery. Ain't that cute? Antique, I bet?'

Dorothy shook her wrist free and, presenting Clapper with the voucher for his taxi ride, said:

'Six shillings, honey. One dollar and twenty cents. That's what it costs you to talk to me!'

Clapper put his hand obediently into an inner pocket and pulled out a very old pound note.

She took the change from her tin safe and, laying it on the counter, announced:

'There you are, son. Six and four are ten, and ten make twenty. Can you count?'

'No,' said Clapper, 'but I'll take your word for it.'

He took the silver up but forgot the ten-shilling note. His leave was just beginning, and he had only the haziest idea of our currency.

'Now, Butch, don't forget the note. The Red Cross won't rob you, but it's a bad habit to get into. Have you had anything to eat?'

'No, ma'am. I knew there was something on my mind.'

'Then run up to the first floor and grab yourself some stew. I'll have you paged when the driver's ready to start. Can I help you, Corporal?'

The corporal, who had been waiting patiently in the queue, edged up to the counter.

'Where do I find out about trains, ma'am?'

'Where do you want to get to?'

'Home.'

'Where's home?'

'Ohio,' grinned the corporal.

'Dandy, honey. I went to school with a girl from Tennessee; that's the nearest I ever got to it. What can I do for you, Airborne?'

Airborne wanted a bicycle. He was tired of the big city and dreamed of the English countryside. Tomorrow was Sunday, and somebody had told him the Red Cross had bicycles

with the name of an American State on each. He came from
Kansas and wanted to leave at seven in the morning. Kay
turned to a mass of papers strewn in front of her.

'A, B, C . . .' she started. 'Ralph Kessler has Alabama.
Sergeant Gene Berg has Connecticut. O.K. honey, we'll
book you for Kansas at 7 a.m. It will be waiting for you
at the door. Now, don't be late.'

'You're a sweetheart,' said Airborne.

He was about to turn away when he changed his mind
and gave a last grateful look at Kay.

'What I like about you, honey,' he said, 'is your smile.'

Brave little Kay! Her smile belied her feelings, but
Airborne could not have guessed her secret.

'Hi, how are you?'

It was Dorothy calling to a young fellow with a bandaged
chin. He was an old friend. He had been in several days
earlier telling Dorothy about his swimming feats. His
bandaged chin gave him rather a pathetic expression and he
seemed to think it called for some excuse, for he muttered
almost inaudibly, 'Testing a jeep—it caught fire!'

'Do you want to see a good-looking boy?' asked
Dorothy, removing the swimmer's cap, thus revealing a
thick crop of straw-coloured hair. While the lad blushed,
Kay took the cap which was on the counter and turned it
over thoughtfully. 'Be careful,' said Dorothy; 'you never
know what these boys hide in their hats.'

The swimmer recovered his headgear and melted away
in the crowd. He doubtless thought that a jeep on fire was
less dangerous than being admired in public.

It was nearly one o'clock. 'Diamonds', the taxi-driver
with twenty-five years' experience of our London streets,
was collecting his passengers for his second grand tour of
the day. He was born in Spitalfields and said he would not
be on duty on Sunday because he was going to spend the
day with his family at Slough—no, not by taxi but in the
train. While Dorothy was paying him off, a boy came up and
asked the way to the Washington.

Dorothy took a sheet of paper to draw him a map, and with her pencil still poised:

'Do you know Piccadilly Circus, son?'

'No, ma'am.'

'Have you seen that boxed-up statue in the middle of the square?'

'Yes, ma'am.'

'Do you know what it's called?'

'No, ma'am.'

'That's Eros, honey.'

The soldier looked puzzled. 'Why, sure,' he said. 'I guess it must be called after the news-reel theatre next door.'

Dorothy threw her hands up in despair. Even she was nonplussed.

'Darling,' she said to Kay, 'you take over from here.' Then turning to me, she added in her rich drawl:

'Come on. Let's go eat somethin'.'

What I admired most about Dorothy Berker was her adaptability. From her seat behind the information counter she could talk back to the boys in their own language—the rich, colourful speech they loved and understood. A moment later she was the hostess who in pre-war days had gathered famous people round her table in Cannes, in Paris, or in New York. But always she kept those soft intonations that were so redolent of her native State. We lunched on the second floor, where Gwen Winingham came over to join us for coffee. Miss Winingham's name was synonymous with the Rainbow. She hailed from the mid-West and her warm handshake was typical of her loyal character.

The most picturesque corner of the Rainbow was the Back Room, which was at its best when it was so crowded that you could hardly breathe, so noisy that you could scarcely hear yourself speak. It had green walls and there were banks of flowers and coloured electric light bulbs round the orchestra which played those transatlantic rhythms which our Allies had brought over with them. There was a shoe-shine parlour and a juke box. The voice of Bing Crosby blended with the clinking of Coca-Cola bottles, and over all there was a haze of violet smoke from American cigarettes.

In a corner of the Back Room stood a desk behind which, perched on the arm of a chair, was a slim dark figure surrounded by a crowd of eager faces. She was Lady Charles Cavendish, well remembered as Adèle Astaire. On the wall there was a painted panel with a blue bird flying away carrying a sealed missive in its beak. A notice read: 'Let Adèle Astaire write home for you.'

This scene in a basement below Shaftesbury Avenue where the afternoon traffic was roaring towards Piccadilly Circus struck a note in my heart. Adèle Astaire was writing busily on a pad. Soon a letter would be speeding across three thousand miles of ocean telling how a boy in khaki, lost in the swirl of London, was thinking of a girl back home. Though Eros had been taken away from his plinth, his spirit was still hovering round the Circus.

At the other end of the half-mile—in Leicester Square— the name of Fred Astaire was written large across the façade of the giant Odeon. His latest film was drawing the Town. Brother and sister could almost reach across the teeming crowds of Coventry Street and shake each other by the hand. It was a new and wonderful partnership. Both were making the boys feel less strange in a strange city.

Adèle Astaire had finished her letter. An enthusiastic G.I. had persuaded her to take the floor with him and dance the boogie-woogie. That boy would be able to tell his folks at home that one Saturday, in London, he had partnered the great Adèle Astaire. The crowds in Shaftesbury Avenue would have given a lot to step down for a few moments into the Back Room and witness this impromptu show.

1944

THE SIEGE OF LONDON

THE SIEGE OF LONDON

THE year 1944 was welcomed in by a terrific crowd in Piccadilly Circus that overflowed into the adjoining streets. A full hour before midnight the police were obliged to divert traffic. As Big Ben tolled the hour and the bells of St Martin-in-the-Fields pealed the New Year in over the heart of London, torches shone on the plinth of Eros and people of all nations sang 'Auld Lang Syne'. Americans and Dutchmen, Poles and Frenchmen joined in the words. This great gathering was unexpected. Our allies from across the seas were, I think, the moving spirit. Londoners since the war had been notoriously chary of giving vent to their feelings in public. On previous occasions New Year's Eve had been rung in more quietly, but this time even the most reserved amongst us were moved by a sense of great things ahead.

On New Year's Day, on my return from lunch, Mr Crouch handed me a small package which had been delivered, he said, by a young man who preferred not to leave his name.

Hurrying into the apartment, I found that Margaret, after having given Bobby and Pouffy their lunch, had put my son to bed for his afternoon nap. My pekinese, mad with joy at my return, started licking the make-up off my face.

Then I remembered the package that I had put with my handbag on the dining-room table. Intrigued by its anonymous messenger I opened it to find to my amazement a magnificent silk square from that famous shop in the

Faubourg St Honoré whose silk squares have a distinction all of their own. The motif was the conquest of England by the Normans—from the Bayeux tapestry. What a strange message! Then my heart began to beat very fast because the gift was from Pierre during one of those dangerous visits he was making clandestinely to Paris and the motif on the scarf was obviously a gentle and kindly allusion to my farm in Normandy about which we had so often talked, sadly, nostalgically, I wondering if I would ever see it again, whether I would ever be reunited with my mother. What a lot of trouble he must have gone to for my sake! I began to tremble a little and even to weep. He had succeeded more often than any other man in these dangerous missions but there was an end to everything. My mind went back to an evening during the previous September.

Pierre had called at the apartment. He did not often come to see me and when he did it was an honour because almost every moment of his day was taken up with plans and conferences at General de Gaulle's headquarters. But I had no sooner opened the door of the apartment that I gave a little cry of surprise. His hair was cropped short in the German way, and I particularly noticed a streak of white in the centre above the forehead. He wore heavily tinted spectacles, and though it was not difficult to recognize him, I felt a shock—and apprehension to see him thus changed.

Pierre was going back. I had no need to ask him. Everything made it all too obvious, and I thought of his wife, brave as she was, and how distressed she must be. We looked at each other and he merely nodded assent. He said something about being unable to leave friends in the lurch. Several leaders of the resistance group in the French capital had been caught lately and the patriots needed somebody from London to reassure them—to show them they were not forgotten. But the third journey was always the most dangerous. He would be hunted remorselessly by the Gestapo, who were well aware of his previous trips and were not likely to be put off for long by this disguise. There was nothing I could say. Not even his family counted when it was a question of what he believed to be his duty. All men worthy of the name are like that. Bobby was asleep in the cot in my bedroom and he asked that I should not wake him. He was rather self-conscious about his Teutonic coiffure, and knew how observant children are. Doubtless also he felt that the child might talk. Though Pierre was as brave as a lion, he was sensitive about his appearance, about the impression he made—and he rather liked my son. He said, to make me feel at ease: 'The child might laugh at me!' As if anybody would have dreamed of laughing at Pierre! There were strange angles in his character. I often heard him say, for instance, how little he could withstand physical pain. Some men are made that way and it has nothing to do with courage. I was to remember this later.

Pierre stayed for about half an hour and he was more charming than ever.

The truth is that I liked him better every time I saw him. He was an extraordinary mixture of what is obstinate and lovable. His fiery character was tinged with gentleness. The previous June he had looked in at a tea-party I was giving for Bobby's birthday, and the two of them had romped as if they had been of the same age. He had asked me to tell him about the small farm at Villers-sur-Mer where I had given birth to Bobby and from which we had to flee at a moment's notice, leaving the lunch uneaten on the kitchen table while the Nazi tanks thundered towards us.

So he never went into the bedroom to say good-bye to Bobby but merely pressed my hand eloquently as if he wanted to put into his handshake all the things he could not say aloud. The next day he was gone. He was supposed to be away three months but of course we had no news, and the best I could do was occasionally to ask the Lady of Paris, if I met her, if everybody in her family was keeping well. It was not that there was any secret between us, but it is all too easy to commit an indiscretion which, in Pierre's case, might have had dire consequences.

So now he had stopped off at this expensive shop in the Faubourg St Honoré to buy me a silk square. We younger women dreamt of discovering real silk squares that to some extent had replaced our lovely pre-war hats. Hats were rare and for special occasions. I had left all my pretty hats in a hatbox with M. Schwenter at the Hôtel Meurice in Paris, who promised to keep them for me till the war was over. Would I ever go back to claim them?

With the silk square there was a letter, not from Pierre, but from the bearer of the gift (no wonder he refused to give Mr Crouch his name!). The letter said in English: 'On behalf of my very good friend, Pierre, I am leaving this parcel he requested me to give you, with his very best wishes for a prosperous and victorious New Year 1944. May I add mine? Pierre will doubtless, upon his return, repeat them himself.'

My emotion was intense. It still is at the thought of it. Consider what it meant to receive a New Year's gift from Paris delivered the same day—or at least the day after. The gift had winged its way over the almost impenetrable barrier dividing the two capitals. Pierre had bought it himself. He may even have packed it that morning. He was alive and well. He was thinking of all his friends in London and obviously planned to be back soon—in a matter of weeks or even days.

I was filled with a new hope.

THE sharp raids of February 1944 broke a lull of nearly three years. The weather was bitterly cold, with occasional snow, but it was gone by morning, leaving a hard frost in the Green Park and a thin coating of ice on the sump.

Nobody was surprised to hear the sirens again, because the newspapers were filled with stories about the Allied raids on Germany. The unknown factor was the extent to which the enemy could go and the improvements he had made in his technique. This uncertainty, added to tiredness and war strain, made many people more nervous than during the battle of London, and when the bombs began to drop near the centre of town, one saw again the early evening trek towards the tube stations. As soon as it became dark a great hush fell over the city.

This mantle of silence was one of the strangest phenomena. One could hear it, yes, actually hear it. On several occasions when I was at home with the curtains drawn, this sudden blanketing fell upon my ears and made me aware that it was now officially night. It was most impressive on the evening following a big raid, when people were still under the domination of fear. One felt a shudder down the spine. There was something about it which was not of this world.

These raids were not at all like those of 1940–1. They were noisier but seldom lasted more than an hour, at any rate in their intensity, whereas in the old days, or rather, in the old nights, the sirens wailed regularly at dusk and did not sound the all clear until half an hour before dawn.

London itself had also changed. It was now crowded with American soldiers, many of whom, only a few months earlier, were pursuing peaceful occupations in city or farm. In addition to this great army from across the Atlantic, there had come into London a tremendous number of people of every sort and kind who had not been through any of the previous raids. The population had therefore to be welded together and tempered before attaining that hardness and stoicism with which it faced the much more terrifying raids of May 1941.

The bombs did not really hit the heart of the town until Sunday, 20th February. Before that we had only seen fires round the perimeter. But on this occasion there was quite a large conflagration in Pall Mall, and one saw other patches of deep red seemingly quite near but more difficult to locate.

That evening, after the sirens sounded, Dorothy Berker rang my bell. She used to consider my apartment as a half-way house between her flat and the basement shelter—safer than her flat and less noisy because it was on the street level, not so desirable as the shelter when a raid was at its height because, in spite of undoubted advantages, the windows were a distinct menace.

Dorothy used to arrive with her lovely mink coat and a big floppy bag filled with her movable treasures. She rolled up her blonde hair above her forehead in the shape of a wave about to break on the foreshore. It was generally not long before we went out into the passage under the clock by the main entrance. Here we would often meet Sylvia, especially if her husband was fire-watching in the City, where he had his office. Sylvia was slim, with finely chiselled features, a host of almost imperceptible freckles and a timid expression. Sylvia's mink coat was very dark and rich, and was almost as lovely as the one Dorothy wore. She spoke with a faint mid-European accent that gave a soft texture to her voice, and she was multilingual. The night porter did not like people to stand in his corridor, and as I had a boxroom in the basement we used to go there, threading our way through the picturesque crowds that came in for shelter from the streets or from adjoining buildings considered less safe than ours. In this way a sort of understanding grew up between us—that when the siren went we three women should forgather.

After the big fire in Pall Mall, we expected the raids to become more violent each night. There was nothing on the Monday, but in the early hours of the Wednesday morning we were wakened by the sirens. After that quite a lot of people started to leave town. I cannot say that I ever felt particularly frightened. Had it not been for Dorothy and Sylvia I might even had remained in the flat sleeping or working according to the hour of the night. As it was, I organized my life differently.

On the Wednesday evening, the sirens sounded at about nine o'clock. Sylvia came down with a young Frenchman who had lately made some adventurous trips to his native

land, from which he came back on this occasion with a bus
ticket and a piece of Paris soap. The close fellowship
between the Allied forces was sometimes confusing, for this
boy wore British uniform and at first I had not realized his
nationality. Dorothy brought along a young compatriot
who was in London for the first time and on whom she had
taken compassion when, earlier in the day, he had called
for her at the Red Cross centre during his twenty-four
hours' leave. She kept open house for friends whose spells
in town were brightened by an illusion of home life. They
heard a woman's voice again, sat in comfortable armchairs
by the fire and ate off real china with silver forks and
spoons. They often brought some contribution to the meal
and occasionally even cooked it themselves. I began to
understand why Dorothy had no time to worry about the
future.

The noise of the rocket guns reverberated above all the
other sounds of the angry night. Sometimes a door would
be blown back on its hinges or the electric light fade out for
a few seconds. Sylvia was momentarily out of sympathy
with the Americans. Her maid in the country was apparently
in love with a Kentucky sergeant, and this warrior ruled
her country house during the week and even slept in her
bedroom, but Sylvia knew that if she raised any objection, the
maid would give notice and she might not find another.
We told her she was lucky to have a maid and even
luckier to have a country house, and she answered:
'Yes, but in the train on Saturday, my husband and I invited
an American flying officer stationed near us to dinner on
Sunday and he did not turn up. You know what it means
to plan a meal these days.' I could see that Dorothy was
about to take up the challenge on behalf of her compatriots
who were so often called to action stations at a moment's
notice, and I was almost glad when the ground shook.
'Did you feel that?' asked Sylvia. 'I'm sure that was a bomb.'
Dorothy offered some American cigarettes and the American
boy put in: 'No, you must have some of mine.' 'They *are*

yours,' answered Dorothy. 'This is the packet you brought me.' Dorothy received quantities of cigarettes, candies, and chewing-gum from her protégés and generally handed these luxuries round. She claimed to have enough chewing-gum to tie up an army.

The night had become quiet and suddenly the all clear sounded in the distance, being taken up by successive stations until the long blast echoed right above our heads. Dorothy and I decided to put her young soldier on his road and to inspect on the same occasion what we could of the night's damage. There were fires all over the town, and one of them was so near to St James's Palace that we felt convinced that by now that historic landmark must be a raging inferno. We crossed the Green Park to the gate by Lancaster House where already we were greeted by the smell of burning wood and the acrid stench of cordite. A band of men was working by glimmering torches and the light of nearby fires at the bottom of St James's Street where it is met at right angles by Pall Mall. Great pieces of masonry and broken glass, charred beams, and red brick encumbered the road, which was filled with water from the snake-like hoses of the firemen. We picked a path warily over all this debris, looking up nervously at the tower of the palace fearing to find it mutilated, but except that the clock, which we must have consulted a thousand times when passing that way, had been defaced and the hands wrenched off, the red-brick palace seemed safe. All the damage was on the other side of Pall Mall, where the insides of many shops were blown into the roadway. Outside one shop a stuffed crocodile lay with jaws wide open in a pool of water. A wild duck had been catapulted from the same establishment, which sold guns and sporting materials, and was perched on a broken bureau, looking down on the crocodile with cold, inanimate eyes. All this, by the flicker of our torch, seemed eerie and unreal. One part of the road was littered with correspondence addressed to a comforts fund, and a knitted jumper, doubtless made by loving hands to keep some sailor warm while on patrol duty, lay there torn and sodden. A motor-car which must have been waiting at the kerb was twisted out of recognition. We picked our way up St James's Street, and when we came level with King Street we had the impression of looking into Dante's Inferno. From St James's Theatre to St James's Square all seemed wreckage and fire. Heavy gilt picture-frames from the shattered establishment of a famous art dealer lay in the middle of the street. Spink's was on fire. The already charred skeleton of Christie's stood out in the fantastic light like a Roman temple. I had seen it burn, all but the bare walls, in one of the great night attacks in 1941. It would have gone now, had it not gone then. Its fate was doubly sealed.

We could but peer in the direction of St James's Square and speculate on the fate of the London Library. The night's savagery appeared to be concentrated as far as the West End was concerned on this centre of art and letters. We walked to the corner of Bond Street where Dorothy and I bade goodnight to our young American boy, leaving him to make his way alone through the dark night in the direction of Oxford Street. We walked silently home, appalled by what we had seen, for though the damage was less spectacular than much of what we had known during the raids of 1940-1, there seemed something particularly wanton in the destruction of books and pictures, tapestries and treasures of a past age.

The next morning was fine and dry and it felt good to be alive. 'Good morning,' said Mr Crouch, the head porter. 'Did you hear about Con?' 'About the doorman who has been away with stomach trouble? No,' I answered. 'He was killed last night with all his family,' said Mr Crouch. 'They were having dinner when two bombs hit the building in Chelsea where they lived. Eighty people lost their lives.'

The day seemed much less fine and I kept on thinking about Con, who used to clean my windows and rub down the mirror. I made a detour by St James's Square to find out exactly what had happened to the library. On my way I met

Mrs Baumer, a friend whose husband was in the Mediterranean. She lived in the neighbourhood, and was too full of her own troubles to give me much news. Her flat had been rendered uninhabitable during the night and she was going off to live with a rich widow near Marble Arch, but she told me about her porter's kittens which were hurled in a basket from the floor to the top of a cupboard where, after this frightening journey through space, the mother cat spent the entire night licking the tiny particles of glass from the paws of her offspring. I believe the unfortunate animal died later from the effects of its devotion. But just then Mrs Baumer was concerned about her own future, though nothing could ruffle her quiet disposition. 'Well, darling,' she drawled. 'Goodbye and give me a ring some time.'

What had happened to the library? The façade was still intact but something warned me that all was not well. I pushed the door open and found myself in a terrible mess of broken glass and torn volumes. The girls who had just arrived were standing round, too awed to speak. Some of them looked like weeping. The secretary, who was firewatching when the bomb fell, had ducked under the counter with his companions. He looked haggard and dazed and said that the explosion had been terrific. A few moments after the sirens had gone, his wife walked over from their flat which overlooked the back of the library to join him, and this may have saved her life, judging by the damage to their home. In the library the hall was more or less intact. The real damage was in the art room where the bust of Thomas Carlyle had been hurled from its niche and decapitated; in a section of the reading room, and amongst the biographies on the third and fourth floors, where a wing of the so-called new building was carried away when the bomb crashed down into a mews. All the books were thrown from the shelves, and what remained of them was covered with white dust. A number of twisted steel girders were holding back a load of rubble and pulverized literature. If one went too near the edge, one overlooked a gaping chasm. When I returned later in the day I found nearly twenty of the girls already at work. Eleanor Rendall, her hair clogged with brick dust and her arms black with dirt, was climbing over the debris with no thought for her safety. 'For thirteen years I have put the biographies away,' she said. 'I must save what I can.'

She showed me the various floors cut open on one side like a doll's house, and when we approached the danger spots, she exclaimed laughing: 'Follow me. I know just how far the floor will bear our weight!' Down in the hall, the white-haired septuagenarian Mr Cox was sitting behind his desk wearing a soft black hat and a white silk scarf, looking as if he were all dressed up to go to the opera. He was aggrieved because the enemy had attacked this part of London which he had known since childhood. 'Have you seen King Street?' he asked.

That night the sirens sounded again—this time just after the nine o'clock news. We had given up the boxroom for the residents' shelter which, for some reason or other, we had not discovered before. It was a large and well-constructed room with several exits designed by experts, and these doors could be opened by a key kept behind glass, which one was supposed to break in case of an emergency. The night porter shepherded his clients into this palatial retreat and left them to sit on the chairs and camp-beds with which the company had furnished it. There were seldom more than a dozen people, for most residents preferred to congregate with the public in the passages.

Dorothy had brought a couple of friends—a good-looking sailor celebrating his twenty-fourth birthday, and a doctor from Philadelphia in uniform.

'And now,' Dorothy said to the sailor, 'it's your birthday today. Remember, you can do just what you like—all the evening. When the raid is over, we'll go up and finish supper.' Then, turning to me: 'And you'll come too, won't you?' She smiled as if recalling something that had amused her during the day, and added: 'You know the way our boys call your ladies of easy virtue "commandos". Lord B.'s son came in with an American friend to the Red Cross this afternoon. He was in uniform, and before leaving, he took off his shoulder-flash with "Commando" embroidered in large letters on it, and gave it to me as a keepsake. You can imagine the howl of delight that went up from all the G.I.s when he pinned it on my dress!' 'Most of your commandos,' put in the doctor in a tone of voice that suggested he knew what he was talking about, 'most of your commandos try to get something extra out of our boys by asking them for five dollars with which to buy new black-out curtains. I reckon that's pretty strange. In the old days they used to ask for a dress or a hat. Even the oldest profession keeps abreast of the times.'

Dorothy laughed. 'I think some of the G.I.s are scared of them,' she said. 'The other night I had been dining with a friend at her house when the sirens went. She was the best-groomed thing I've seen since leaving New York and made me feel I'd like to take my hat out of the mothballs. But she lived on the seventh floor and that was too high up for me during an air raid, so I left her and looked round for a taxi. By the time I had walked to the bottom of the street, with the shrapnel falling pretty fast, I came across a couple of G.I.s going in the same direction. "I'm from the Red Cross," I said. "Where are you boys going to?" "To the 'Washington', ma'am." "Then take me with you," I answered. "I shall feel a lot better with a male escort." They brought me right here to the main entrance, but just as we were parting I felt that it would be a kindly gesture to repay their trouble, so I began: "If you boys would like to come up a moment, I'll make you a cup of real American coffee." You should have seen the way they ran for their lives. They certainly were not taking any risks with strange women!'

Dorothy, who was in excellent spirits, went on, 'You know how the boys come to ask me all sorts of questions?

One of them attracted my attention. He was six foot three, had a hare lip and a lisp, and scarcely enough flesh to cover his bones. I noticed him from quite a distance, for he seemed unable to walk like other men, but shuffled like a country bumpkin. His army clothing seemed only to fit him where it touched him—it hung limply as from the boughs of a tree. As he looked over the edge of my counter, he appeared absolutely miserable. "Are you Dorothy?" he asked. "Yes, what can I do for you?" "I heard a lot about you. You are mighty pretty." "That's very nice of you." He paused a moment and went on: "I ahm not good-looking. I have a hare lip and I ahm not happy. I got a girl and I can never tell her I like her." "Now, come, young man, you should make a list of the words you are unable to say." He dismissed this trite observation, and queried: "I wonder if the A.P.O. is open?" "Oh," I answered, "if you have a letter to post and it's been censored, I'll be glad to mail it for you." "No, ma'am, I got to send seven hundred and ninety dollars home." "Holy goodness! Where did you get seven hundred and ninety dollars?" "That ain nothing. I have sent home mighty near eight thousand dollars since I have been in the European theatre of operations." "But where have you made all that money?" "I run a little crap game." "That's an awful lot of money, young man." "Yes, ma'am, and it is money where I come from, but I can't tell mommer anythin' about it, because we is foot-washin' Baptists."

'Tears rolled down his cheeks. "My mommer thinks I don't do anythin' she don't want me to do, and I has increased her allotment to fifty dollars a month, but she writes me: 'Son, don't send me all that money because I don't think you have enough to go up to town with.'" He paused a moment and continued: "Yes, ma'am, when I get back home, I'se goin' to be the biggest man in the town and I'se goin' to buy up everythin', but I reckon my mommer worries about me. Well, I'se been thinkin' that as you come from our home state, you could write to my mommer, ma'am. You would pull a lot of weight with mommer. It would be worth a lot if you would write to her." "Yes, son, I'll certainly write to your mamma," I answered, "but I must stick to the truth and so all I can say is that you don't dance and you don't smoke. I'll do that." "Thank you kindly, ma'am. My mommer will be pleased."'

'There go the sirens!' broke in the sailor.

We took the lift up to the seventh floor, going out for a moment on the roof to see the results of the nocturnal attack. Once again there were fires rising in all directions, fanned by a bitterly cold wind. A group of people whose features were hardly distinguishable in the darkness stood awestruck on the edge of the parapet. They were trying to locate the various fires by plotting them in relation to known landmarks. 'Piccadilly runs along there,' an officer was saying as he pointed with his cane. 'The tall building on the right is the Ritz, and on the other side is Devonshire House. That big blaze must be just beyond Piccadilly Circus.' 'No,' answered somebody, 'that fire must be at least two miles away.' Distantly one heard the clanging of a fire engine, and there floated across the roof the smell of burning paper and charred wood. There was not, however, the feeling that had choked us so often of a city in agony. These conflagrations were terrible to behold; they represented death and suffering, but they were obviously under control and not sufficiently numerous to put the town in danger. 'Come,' said Sylvia who had followed us up. 'I don't like to watch this.' She probably echoed the feeling of all of us. Below us, the streets were strangely empty, but far away a car could be heard changing gear and gathering speed; a deep voice called out and was answered; a soldier began to sing out of tune.

WHILE in the country violets and primroses must have been carpeting the hedgerows and the woods, Bobby, Pouffy and I were inhaling the fine brickdust of demolished houses and the acrid smoke of burning wood. I was beginning to feel a little guilty about my small son, wondering also if I myself were not on the verge of a breakdown. I kept practically open house for anybody who liked to come in for lunch, and though this was highly satisfactory, helping by this family atmosphere to keep us all sane, it meant infinite queueing and cajoling for food, and I only managed to keep going by a huge interest in the enormous drama that was being played out all around me and by my determination to do everything I could to influence in the right direction the formative years of my growing child.

At the height of the February–March raids, however, I decided to take Bobby and Pouffy away for a week if only I could find some suitable place in the country. After four and a half years of war the problem had difficulties. We were always being asked not to travel for our pleasure and there were not many hotels that were likely to welcome our presence. The sea had disappeared behind barbed wire and the west country, where the first apple blossom was doubtless to be seen, was filled with engines of war for the coming invasion.

I went one morning to Cook's in Berkeley Street where an assistant asked me what part of the country I had in mind, and when I told him that this was immaterial but that I would like a country inn with some woods and a river, he began being very helpful. Then I said: 'I have a child aged four and a half.' His face fell. I was no longer the desirable traveller. He could not have looked more embarrassed if I had told him that I was suffering from yellow fever. His attempts to soften the blow were pathetic. 'Most hotels refuse to accept children,' he said. 'They make a noise and spoil the furniture.'

It was true that I had little furniture in my apartment and that Bobby's chief joy was to write and draw on the painted walls of the drawing-room.

We started all over again and by this time a queue was forming behind me, but there was an inn in the Wye

Valley where the owners might consider the proposition if it were put to them tactfully on the telephone. A few moments later the assistant returned with a smile on his tired face. 'I've fixed it,' he announced. He asked me what class I intended to travel and was moving towards the ticket counter when I said: 'And please give me a dog ticket.' 'A dog ticket?' he exclaimed. 'Did I hear you say a dog ticket?' I felt as if I had done something wrong. He went on: 'The owners positively refuse to take dogs. There's not an hotel, an inn, or a lodging house on my list which allows its guests to bring their pets.' 'It's a very small dog,' I pleaded, 'a pekinese.'

The queue was becoming larger and the assistant was toying with the papers, having come to the end of his patience. 'You will have to make a choice, Madam.' 'I shall take the dog,' I announced with determination. 'As you please,' he said, 'but the inn is several miles from the nearest railway station and you may find yourself without a lodging for the night.'

The next morning, with Bobby and Pouffy, I took the express to Gloucester and drove to an inn on the flank of a mountain overlooking the famous salmon river. Two women owned it and everything was so gay, so neat, so brightly scrubbed and polished that I knew there would be no trouble. The maid with her dark hair, her well-ironed cap, her stooping back and worn hands hurried out to fetch our bags from the car. She told us in a cockney accent that the partners were having their afternoon nap and would be down in time for tea. While showing us a large bedroom above the parlour, she told me she had been bombed out of her home in London. The air was sweet with country smells, and the sun was covering the opposite bank of the fast-running river with a cloak of gold. Wisps of smoke rose from all the cottages, and the trees were already green with bursting buds. This was spring in all its magnificence. Bobby and Pouffy were panting to explore this new world which seemed to them greener, fresher, larger and much more

mysterious than the London parks which until now had
constituted the scene of their daily walks.

Dora, one of the two partners, was tall and portly with a
complexion that looked as if it had been scrubbed with soap
and water, and she wore a bright red knitted shawl over her
ample shoulders. She sailed towards the roaring fire from
the direction of the bar and held out a large, firm hand. She
said that her partner Esther would be down soon.

I had never seen more lovely country. My mother-in-law
was right in blaming me for not having bought a farm in
England. Had I bought one here I would never have
become temporarily a refugee. The top of the mountain
was full of surprises. The mighty trees of the Forest of
Dean arched above our heads. There were crags and clear-
ings planted with young trees and heather; there were farms
upon which one came unexpectedly and where the children
had the accents of Limehouse or Barking, for they were
evacuees of four years' standing who had grown more
accustomed to the country than the city. There were cottages with white façades decorated with japonica; ducks and
geese in fields no larger than a handkerchief and surrounded
by stone walls.

The evenings in the bar were enchanting. Both Dora and
Esther were admirable hosts. They had met when nursing
in the same London hospital. After leaving hospital work,
Dora was for some time a buyer for a large store in Cardiff
where her good sense and knowledge of what women
wanted made her so successful that she travelled widely
on the Continent, choosing dresses and hats, materials and
lampshades. The inn was a wartime experiment.

At the door of this gay country inn knocked one dark
night a young couple brought from the station by Matthews,
the local taxi-driver. Gloria, the maid, had just brought
Esther her nightly cup of tea. Two American soldiers were
dozing against each other by the roaring fire, in front of
which two spaniels were lying with their paws stretched

out on the carpet. Matthews followed the newcomers into the room, and when he had set down the luggage he rubbed his numbed hands and, as an habitué of the house, passed behind the counter to pour himself out a pint of ale. Dora rose to make her guests welcome. The man was very dark. His overcoat collar was turned up and he was shivering. Sparse of build, his complexion was white and tired, the complexion that a man has after a sleepless night, when the colour has gone from the cheeks and the eyes are rimmed. The young woman was tall, elegant and beautifully slim. She wore a small felt hat which suited her large, expressive eyes and olive skin, almost Spanish in texture. Her wide shoulders and the absence of hips gave her a boyish figure. What struck me most was a sad aloofness which attracted all one's attention until one began to feel that it gave character to the features, and then one ceased to notice it. She wore a grey Persian lamb coat over a grey suit, and shoes with solid heels, and she carried a crocodile bag with her initials on it. Dora took them to their room and it was some time before they reappeared, the man to sit timidly on a high stool by the bar, the woman to edge at our behest near the fire where we guessed she would be glad to warm herself after the journey. The conversation lagged a little in deference to the new arrivals who had a mid-European accent which we found difficult to locate. They merely told us that they had been bombed out of the apartment they had recently taken near Paddington, where the raids just then were particularly vicious. They were in bed at the time, and though the bomb did no great damage to the apartment, it carried away the staircase, leaving the occupants in mid air so that the fire brigade was obliged to run up a ladder, down which they climbed to safety. Homeless and unwilling to leave London until they could salvage what remained of their furniture and other possessions, they slept every night in tube stations, where they found the platforms crowded not only with Londoners but also with Americans billeted in houses that were not particularly safe when high explosives and incendiaries were falling. After a week of this nomad existence the young couple decided to gather up what remained of their belongings and seek a respite in the heart of the country; the husband would return to London the following day while his wife recuperated, leaving him to look out for a new home. We appreciated their desire to go to bed early and enjoy the comfort of a bath and clean sheets for the first time since their apartment was bombed.

The next day, after the husband had gone back to London, I was sitting in the lounge knitting, Pouffy curled up on my lap. Lunch was over and the house, as usual at this hour, was very quiet. Bobby was asleep in the bedroom and the partners were having their afternoon nap. The young woman came in and, drawing up a chair by the fire, said to me: 'May I call you by your Christian name, Madeleine? Everybody in the inn seems to do so. My name is Inge.' 'Of course,' I answered. 'Inge? Surely that is Scandinavian?' 'Yes,' she answered. 'Inge is short for Ingeborg. But I am not a Scandinavian. I am German and I was born in Berlin.'

She had blurted out the information as if anxious to get it off her mind, but she said something about her pent-up longing to open out her heart to another young woman, and now that we were more or less the only guests in this homely inn, she had felt she could take the risk. So after lunch she had waited till the partners had gone up to their rooms and till all the men had gone about their business, so that we could be alone. As I love to listen to the confidences of other women, I smiled and went on knitting, unwilling to disturb her train of thought. She stroked Pouffy and said:

'I must begin by telling you that, though my father was Aryan in the true Nazi sense, my mother was a Jewess. They were wealthy and I was born within a stone's throw of the Unter den Linden where we had a lovely home. When I came into the world, my father, seeing my blue eyes and my light-brown hair, called me Ingeborg, but as I grew older my hair became dark so that the appellation suited me less well.'

She went on to tell me something of her youth. Like most wealthy girls she spent a lot of her time riding and swimming, and took holidays in Switzerland and in Austria, and had it not been for the regime of the swastika, she would doubtless have had an enviable future because, being an only child, she was heiress to a great fortune.

When the Nazis came into power, her father might have saved himself by abandoning his family but he did not, and Inge said with an almost girlish simplicity: 'You see, my father was still in love with my mother.' And so her father not only remained loyal to her but spent all his time helping others to escape, and eventually he was arrested and thrown into a concentration camp. Inge had just received news from her mother, who was in Switzerland, that he had been tortured to death.

Shortly after their marriage, Inge and her husband tried to leave Germany by way of Hamburg. Her father had managed to give them Italian passports and they hoped to find a ship to take them to safety because, though war was not yet declared, they were not allowed to leave the country. The persecution of their race had already started. If, in Berlin, they went to the theatre, a café or a night club, they ran the risk of being caught in a police sweep. They accordingly stayed in the small apartment which Inge's parents had taken, and at night the men took turns to remain fully dressed in the hall, waiting for the knock at the door which would spell their doom.

At Hamburg while waiting for the ship to sail, Inge and her husband stayed at an hotel where, during the evening, they found the corridor filled with S.S. men. At first, so intense was the nightmare of persecution that they thought these men might have gathered to arrest them, but on second thoughts, it seemed unlikely that a whole detachment of special police would be looking for two humble fugitives. The waiter who brought them supper gave them the reason for this display of force. Himmler was occupying the adjoining suite. His personal bodyguard was in the corridor. Whatever relief they felt at this discovery was lessened by the knowledge that they would have to remain hidden in their rooms until Himmler's departure. Not only the corridor would be guarded but also the lifts, the foyer, and even the streets round the hotel.

When at last they boarded the ship they had believed would take them to safety, they discovered that it was going on a Strength through Joy cruise, and that all the passengers were ardent Nazis.

They returned to the family in Berlin where Inge's father, still at liberty, was now doing more than ever to provide passports, clothes and money to all those who had a chance to escape, and it was he who suggested that they should try to reach London by the ordinary aeroplane service, making use of the Italian passports he had given them. Because of bad weather the plane was unable to go farther than Düsseldorf, and Inge and her husband, alarmed at this unexpected change in their plans, risked taking the pilot into their confidence. He gave them the address of an hotel where he claimed they would have the chance of passing unnoticed. His advice might have proved a trap. They could not tell how real was his sympathy. To make matters worse, the whole town was beflagged. Hitler himself was due to arrive the next morning to attend the funeral of the German diplomat recently murdered in Paris. The body of the murdered Nazi was being brought back to stage a gigantic demonstration.

The young couple returned to Berlin. They eventually fled by way of Switzerland and after many more adventures reached England.

She and I became friends and together with Bobby and Pouffy went for long walks—along the valley where the river flowed past thick woods in which heavy carts made tracks in the black, damp earth; where the woodcutters made picturesque fires which smelt of pine and ash; where white and purple violets peeped from the moss-covered banks covered with wild strawberries, and where one could stand amidst the undergrowth and watch the silver-bellied salmon jump the rapids—and then there was the 'mountain'. In London, wheeling the pram with Bobby, the pekinese and my shopping, I used to walk for miles through the streets, often past houses that had only just collapsed, with Anne of Brittany. How amazingly in times of war can two young women open out their hearts, telling each other without concealment the things that hurt, the scars, the anxieties and distress. I never again rediscovered so poignantly such feminine friendships that with the return of peace were generally veiled by polite reticence. These I knew when London was under fire had a strange, haunting quality that I now become nostalgic for.

We climbed up the 'mountain' by little paths that zig-zagged between the villas above the inn, and where Bobby made friends with a donkey whose owner in the days of Queen Victoria, so he told us, wore a red tunic. One could also climb by more rugged ascents farther along the valley, clambering in town shoes and in tight skirts over rocks and tree stumps, swinging from ash to birch, wedging a foot against a clump of heather, all of which delighted Bobby and the little dog and laddered our precious silk stockings. The view from the top repaid our exertions. The swift river now seemed only a ribbon. It was crossed once or twice a day by a punt tied by a rope to a cable stretching from bank to bank.

Inge confided in me that before the war the English branch of her family had often been their guests in Berlin, sometimes remaining for long periods and being magnificently entertained. When as a refugee Inge had arrived, self-conscious and ashamed, in this country she had immediately gone to see her kinsmen. After the first few times they had cooled and she now thought that her presence was painful to them. Like many others who had not experienced personally the horrors of the Nazi persecution, the degradation of racial laws, the tortures of the concentration camp, they often accused her of exaggeration. Some of them, Jews themselves, gave the impression of being anti-

Semitic. She was surprised and shocked, and ending by finding herself out of sympathy with their views had broken off relations.

She was restless and haunted by the fear of persecution; she was a soul without the hope of Christian belief or any satisfactory religion of her own. She had seen too much of the tragedy of her race to wish to bring children into the world who might be called upon to suffer as she and hers had suffered but the presence of Bobby softened her.

There was nothing in her features to betray her origin. To me she was lovely and I was madly jealous of her beautiful eyes and slim body. I would gladly have changed places physically with her. She was the sort of girl I imagined that men would immediately fall in love with. She was eternally aware, however, that she was both a German and half Jewish, and she claimed that as soon as this fact became known strangers would move away from her, as if she had some infectious disease. Her youth, her beauty, her feminine charm could not weigh in the balance against a tortured mind.

We had reached a spot half way up the mountain where four paths met—a picturesque place, heavily wooded, with just above it a house with green shutters and a red roof. A pine tree stood at each corner of the sombre garden. Bobby used to say that it was the house of a wicked fairy. He had been brought up on Grimms' fairy tales. He half expected to see gnomes popping out of the box hedge. We were resting here after the long climb when suddenly we heard in the clear evening air the strains of an old German folk-song which, in its English adaptation, was being sung by four little girls on their way home from school. Inge listened attentively, and I could see that she had been wafted back into her own childhood, for sentimentally she remained a German girl. Who could suppose otherwise?

We talked, of course, about clothes, about the house a young married woman dreams of owning, about the beautiful linen she would stock in the cupboards, about her kitchen, about the food she liked to cook, and that elusive thing—feminine happiness. There was so much that we could understand in each other. At heart we had both wanted such simple things, the things that every woman really yearns for. We had both, at a certain moment in our lives, felt the carpet being ripped from under our feet. We had both lost a house, lovely clothes and—a country. It didn't really seem to matter much on which side of the fence we had been. That was a man's affair.

She told me about the London flat made uninhabitable by the bomb. She and her husband had taken it in the hope that at last they would have a place of their own. They had welcomed it like a haven for their wandering, unsatisfied souls, where they could discuss their problems in peace without fearing what others might think or say. But their apartment was not friendly to them. The first letter they received was from Inge's mother in Switzerland announcing the death of her father. A few days later they went to dine with friends, and on their return discovered that burglars had broken in. They took all Inge's silk stockings and five of her suits, leaving only ones she had made herself. They left her lingerie, her handkerchiefs and the silver, but took her perfume, some bracelets she had brought back with her from Berlin, all the sugar, a dozen tins of sardines. The police gave them no hope of catching the thieves but the Board of Trade gave Inge thirty clothes coupons, and the insurance gave them some money which Inge was now taking a childish pleasure in spending. The bombing a few days later finished up their home. Once more they became wandering souls, knocking from door to door for a night's rest. And yet Inge, when we talked together, responded like a flower opening its petals in the warm sunshine of a summer's day. I returned to town a few days later, sad to leave Inge behind.

WHEN, towards the end of March, there was still no news of Pierre, the rumour went round that all was not well.

At first we took no notice of it, but one day when Anne of Brittany came to our flat, we told her what we had heard and asked her to make inquiries.

The following morning the telephone rang and Anne said:

'It's true, Madeleine. I'll meet you at the usual place in the Green Park at midday.'

At the appointed hour I went to the Green Park, where Anne was sitting on a hard green chair facing the sump. The sun was shining gloriously—one of the rare fine days in that wet, miserable spring. The weather seemed to mock our grief. Anne said:

'There are several versions of the story. We know that Pierre left Paris a short time ago for Brittany where he was to cross the Channel by sea, bringing with him a very important person. It appears that they had actually pulled out some distance from the coast when they ran into a storm and were obliged to turn back. The Gestapo was waiting for them. Pierre would have been able to swallow his poison pill but he was not willing to abandon his charge, who was elderly.

'They were taken to the prison at Rennes. I am not sure what happened here, but later the Gestapo escorted Pierre to Paris for interrogation and you know what that means. He was too big a catch not to be tortured mercilessly.'

One morning the Lady of Paris telephoned Anne to say that she had grave news about her husband, and later in the day, when they met, she admitted knowing everything. Pierre had ended by jumping into the courtyard from the fifth floor of the prison of Fresnes. His spine was broken and both his legs fractured.

He had asked to be cremated and stipulated that the ashes should be placed in the family vault at Père Lachaise. He was identified by the lock of white hair above his forehead. His real name was Pierre Brosselette.

SINCE General Eisenhower made the U.S. military police

wear white helmets, white belts and white gaiters, these well-turned-out men who drove their jeeps with easy skill through the traffic, or stood informatively at street corners, or strode in couples up and down Piccadilly, had become a picturesque part of the wartime London scene. The G.I.s called them 'snowdrops', not that the military police drooped their heads, but coincidence made them blossom out in white when the first snowdrops of the year were to be found in the more sheltered corners of Hyde Park.

The 787th M.P. Battalion had its headquarters half way down Piccadilly in what was once the Junior Constitutional Club. This building was not what it used to be. The windows were blown out and the exterior looked shabby, but it certainly retained something of its Victorian grandeur. The Americans could still think of it in terms of Sherlock Holmes and hansom cabs. Sweet winds blew across from the Green Park bringing, on a spring morning when the wind was right, the scent of the may. Though the M.P.s had not been in town very long they had already learned a good deal about London, and every now and again I used to see them bringing out their street guides to answer a query, just as our own policemen used to do before the war.

The white-helmeted Americans became more than ever in evidence when so many of the Allied troops left town to take up their stations for the great invasion of the Continent. Indeed, the West End took on quite a different air, and with the exception of a few generals with red tabs and some high-ranking naval officers, all of whom were doubtless engaged in important conferences in Whitehall, the city appeared to have been handed back to what remained of the civilian population.

Londoners, blinking in the sunshine of those last few days of April, looked up into the blue sky when the drone of aeroplanes was heard and asked themselves whether 'it' was for today or tomorrow, this week or next. We all had our theories, our rumours and particular pieces of gossip.

The great question-mark hung heavily over the city. But this spring was one of hope.

There were some perfectly glorious mornings towards the end of April—mornings when the sky was absolutely blue. On such a morning, a little after nine, I turned into Piccadilly from Whitehorse Street to find two long lines of white-helmeted Americans drawn up in the Green Park. These men, whom I soon recognized as the 787th Battalion, were facing Piccadilly, and the Stars and Stripes floated impressively in the breeze. The band, on a lawn a little to the rear, started to play as I crossed the street, and this was the signal for the battalion to wheel to the right and march in that direction. Soon the whole battalion was parading under the trees, making a martial picture in pastoral surroundings.

The sun glittered on the brass and the grass was fresh and tender. In the distance a clump of cherry trees made a splash of white blossom, recalling the orchards where the invasion forces were now gathering in mighty array. The foliage of the hawthorns was several shades deeper than that of the stately chestnuts; the London plane trees were still garlanded with last year's blackened seed balls caught up in the boughs which from a distance appeared leafless, though on looking closer one saw that they were speckled with green.

In the hollow, the mountain ash was putting on its spring garb. The elms and the poplars were only just beginning to wake out of their long winter sleep and had not yet joined this symphony of green, but already a distant line of barbed wire was being hidden by a cloak of sprouting shoots pushing upwards through the damp soil and stretching their arms bravely over the unsightly prickles. The scent of lilac was about, brought to us probably from the white and mauve blossoms which were just beginning to unfold in the gardens of those once stately mansions that run from Arlington House to the Mall. Yes, indeed, this military parade was set in the most peaceful and pastoral surroundings. The white helmets and the white belts and gaiters gave these men a picturesqueness that reminded one of the white breeches of the Napoleonic guard. A small crowd stood under a leafy chestnut, watching the proceedings; their expressions denoted that content of mind which one associates with the happy watchers of a cricket match on the village green. A butcher's boy was leaning against his bicycle. Four French gendarmes who might have sauntered across from the Champs-Elysées stood beside a U.S. officer who had probably brought them along. An elderly man carrying a cauliflower partially wrapped up in an old newspaper, a Norwegian in battledress and two Jack Tars joined the crowd. An American woman of my acquaintance, who was taking a short cut across the park with her daughter, stopped to allow her heart to swell with pride. 'Mr Dash', she said to me, mentioning a well-known American author, 'should write a story about this for Washington, but he's never out of bed at this hour.' Suddenly the strains of 'The Star-spangled Banner' brought everybody to attention, the military people in the crowd springing smartly to the salute. What a lovely morning! What an impressive picture of sturdy American youth parading on foreign soil. Even the butcher's boy had let his bicycle fall on the ground, and there he stood, as smartly as any, impressed by the solemnity of the occasion.

Big Ben struck ten. The M.P.s were marching up and down the lawn. Traffic in Piccadilly was so sparse that a bus travelling west bowled past at a splendid rate. One of our more famous West End tramps—a wild-looking man, but in reality the most philosophic of souls, with a mop of unruly black hair, who wore a frock coat and carried a raincoat over his left arm—was limping along with the aid of a knotty stick. From time to time he would stop and look wistfully at the Americans in the park.

Workmen had placed a tall ladder against the façade of the In and Out Club. They were starting to repair the damage done three years ago during a night raid. A little farther along I came upon the peculiar music of our London streets. The lean man who plays the ambulating piano so well was striking the keys with extra vigour as if resentful of the competition from the brass band in the park. His bemedalled companion was shaking a couple of pennies in a well-worn cap, asking for charity. They were soldiers of the 1914 war.

In the afternoon (it was Saturday), the shopkeepers deserted Shepherd Market, leaving their cats to sleep contentedly behind the plate glass. The itinerant newspaper vendor shuffled along with little hope of selling any more papers until he turned into Piccadilly. The public-houses would not be open for another two hours; the very smart luncheon club, where the other day a business man had paid £48 19s to entertain three colleagues for lunch, had finished until Monday and the chairs were stacked on the tables; the milkman had ended his second round and his pony cart was clattering away down Hertford Street; a strange quiet hung over the main street less than two hundred yards in length, and the garrulous but kind-hearted porter of the small block of flats opposite the hairdresser's, finding nobody worthy of gossip, had disappeared indoors with a pail of water and a scrubbing brush to clean the steps which led to the basement. Even the newsagent had locked up his premises; he generally went to the pictures on Saturday afternoon and then treated himself to dinner at the Corner House. The wealthy residents of the big block of flats had mostly gone to the country because spring was in the air. As I hurried through the labyrinth of narrow streets, I noticed that the neighbourhood was not quite as deserted as it had appeared at first sight. A neat figure standing motionless in an alley under the creaking sign of the village barber revealed the existence of an ancient calling which flourished even after the shops were closed. An almost imperceptible flicker of the eyelids gave that sign of neighbourly recognition according to those of us who were accepted as bona fide villagers. I reciprocated with a smile. There were two French girls who were nearly always together, one of them from the Basque country, dark and pretty who wore the prettiest hats to perfection, as indeed did her friend. Both would have been taken in pre-war days for elegant middle-class Parisian women, even a little prim and haughty. What distinguished them in wartime London was the fact that they were so smartly dressed and wore hats, sometimes even a little perky veil to add brilliance to their dark eyes. Most of us, though we might not have ceased thinking secretly about lovely things, would not have dared, even though we might have had coupons and money to buy new clothes. The market had become, at night and over the week-end, a recognized place for this traffic, which was still looked upon with a benevolent eye both by parliament and the police. Neither was it a speciality of any one country. There were Italian girls, Maltese, a Polish girl who had a passion for dogs and cats, and quite a number of English girls, the different nationalities keeping very much to themselves, a few of them rich enough to own property and live, when off duty (which was seldom), in style. On the whole the market was very peaceful; one seldom heard of drunkenness or brawls. The war had produced an extraordinary neighbourliness born of a complete uncertainty about the future. We would be aware, on the other hand, that the coster whose innocent-looking barrow was parked by the telephone booth had more to sell than he would have liked a stranger to believe—that the solitary cabbage on top of the tarpaulin was only a blind and that, by the odour of citrus fruit which pervaded the market, one might be pardoned for supposing that under the tarpaulin there were oranges and lemons. There was a fortune teller we girls sometimes consulted who wore ornamental hats with tassels and acorns. She was invariably dressed in what had once quite obviously been a blue velvet curtain; she placed circular red blobs on her cheeks like those the toymakers put on dolls, and she painted her lips to resemble an ace of hearts, but she owned a pair of ravishing eyes which any girl would have envied. As she knew all the

THE SIEGE OF LONDON

gossip we consulted her not only to know the future but also the present and the past.

As May came to an end a great change was to be seen in London. The fighting men of all the different nations disappeared from the streets, and even the Whitsun bank holiday had an unnatural look about it. The theatres and restaurants began to fear (without reason) that the boom was at an end. Each day that passed without big news was something of a surprise.

Many of our friends from Occupied Europe gave their views of where the invasion was to take place. The Belgians gave excellent reasons why their coast should be spared and the Bretons were equally convinced that their part of the world was quite unsuitable. They were looking forward enthusiastically to D-day on the condition that the landing did not take place anywhere near their own homes. The tussle between a desire to see the war enter a new phase, and a natural fear that their loved ones might be murdered in the process, was only human.

The first week in June was charged with expectancy and married women were a little jumpy because there was no mail from their menfolk stationed on the south coast. They were no longer able to write direct. On Tuesday morning, 6th June, I was wakened early by a telephone call from the desk of the London *Evening News* asking what the coast was like between Le Havre and Caen. They knew that my small farm was situated half way between these two cities. 'What makes you ask?' I queried. 'The invasion has started,' came the reply.

I had received a Red Cross card from my mother telling us that after bidding farewell to us on the quayside at St Malo during that fateful summer of 1940, instead of returning to Villers-sur-Mer, she had gone first to Paris then to Versailles. This, to some extent, had set my mind at rest.

When later we were re-united she blamed me for not having sent her a similar card through the Red Cross and I never quite forgave myself for this. If the invasion beaches had really been opposite my little farm, the farmhouse would certainly have been obliterated. In fact, as everybody was soon to learn, they were to be some twenty miles to the west of it, between the River Orne and the Cotentin.

Londoners, while these tremendous events were taking place, continued grimly to carry on their business, but one Thursday morning something happened to make them aware that the town might once again come under fire.

At about two o'clock we were wakened by a terrific burst of anti-aircraft fire which ended with a mighty explosion that rocked Carrington House. We leapt out of bed. Then all was quiet—curiously so, because generally these salvoes went on for quite a time, being taken up successively by other batteries until the noise died down. With daylight everybody talked about the flying bombs, and we gathered that the explosion we heard had been caused by one of these breaking up in mid air. Towards midday the Home Secretary gave the first news to the House of Commons that the enemy had begun to use pilotless aircraft against southern England, and the public was warned that, until further notice, the missiles would be fired at by our anti-aircraft guns.

For some time friends who owned an estate in Kent had been asking me to bring the child down for a week-end. I now accepted their invitation. They lived in a large house surrounded by about two hundred and fifty acres of farm-land high above Sevenoaks. The place was aptly known as Highfield and adjoined Dunstall Priory, the estate of the poet Lord Dunsany, who sang its praises in verse. We arrived on a boisterous June day with occasional sunshine but with blasts of chill winds. I had looked forward to this as an interlude away from the atmosphere of war. I could not have guessed that I was to see for the first time what happened when a flying bomb cut out and exploded on the ground.

We walked across a lawn golden with buttercups and shaded with copper beeches, and into a wood where hazels grew. Our host's dog ran ahead, and Bobby, enchanted with the scene, kept on discovering some new wonder. The flying bomb had fallen and exploded just before our arrival. We were being taken to see the result. There was a cottage to be looked at and a coppice of young trees.

We were just leaving the wood and climbing over a low gate when we suddenly noticed the undergrowth strewn with green leaves. This was a phenomenon that not even the worst gale could produce. Imagine green leaves, nearly a foot in depth—leaves of every tree on the borders of the wood, not brown and curly as in autumn, but young and tender in all their June strength. We bent down to pick some up. They might have been blown there by some giant, puffing with all his might. But we saw no broken branches yet—only leaves and more leaves, and soon they were up to the hem of my skirt. Then we came upon what was once a coppice, but now looking for all the world like a stretch of burnt heath on which there were a few charred stubs. It was circular in shape, but in the centre of it lay a young rabbit without a head. Beyond this desolation, stretching away towards the violet hills, was the coppice as it should have been—sturdy young trees about four feet high. Sir Herbert Cohen was tramping ahead of us down the hill, his wife, Bobby and I some paces behind. We came upon some twisted metal—all that remained of a flying bomb which only a few hours earlier had whistled over the roof of the house.

'We call this Magpie Bottom,' Sir Herbert was saying. 'When Dean Inge was a young man, he used to leave the deanery of St Paul's Cathedral on a summer afternoon and take the train at Blackfriars to Shoreham station to walk across the inland downs as far as Wrotham, where he caught the train back to town. As he approached Magpie Bottom, he would see the chimneys of our house—the only sign of human habitation—and he always wondered who lived in that house until, much later, we became close friends.'

'When our boys were young', put in Lady Cohen, 'they would make "Mr Dean" help them with odd jobs about the farm. I remember Nigel saying to him: "Please, Mr Dean, help us hoist a ladder."'

The lane we entered was garlanded with honeysuckle. From time to time we were overtaken by American lorries driven by Negroes from Mississippi—swarthy men beaming at the wheel in this Kentish countryside.

My husband worked for a time at the Ministry of Production and on Sunday mornings he used to walk across Green Park and St James's Park to his office near Storey Gate where he worked before lunch. When it was fine I would dress Bobby in his little blue coat and they would go off together.

On this particular Sunday morning, it had been raining and the sky was overcast but the child was anxious to accompany his father all the same, and it struck me that it might give him an appetite for lunch. They had not been at the office long, Bobby sitting at a desk near his father, drawing on a pad with coloured pencils, before they began to hear flying bombs droning over the roof. At first they took no notice, but just after eleven o'clock, when the church bells had stopped ringing, the roar of one of these pilotless planes came ominously near, growing in intensity every second. My husband took the child by the hand and ran into the passage. The noise was now deafening and my husband knelt down, shielding his son's head. The missile appeared to be headed straight for the roof and the child, frightened for the first time, clutched his arms, crying: 'I love you. I love you.' There was a terrific crash and the building shook. Then a heartrending silence which lasted about thirty seconds, quickly followed by the sound of people running into the street.

The bomb had fallen on the adjacent Guards Chapel which, all but one wall, had collapsed, leaving a mass of ruins from which floated a cloud of white dust. The bomb must have grazed the chimney of the building in which my husband and Bobby were sheltering. The worshippers in the Guards Chapel were buried under the masonry and the explosion wrecked hundreds of windows in the neighbourhood. A young girl, who was crossing the Park at the time, ran about as if demented, with twigs and leaves in her auburn hair. She was the daughter of the Ministry's housekeeper.

The news of the catastrophe in which so many gallant people lost their lives spread rapidly and cast a gloom over London, for it was the first major tragedy occasioned by this new weapon in the heart of the town.

The flying bombs started coming over incessantly day and night. They produced terrific blast and we decided to sleep in the shelter of Carrington House, mostly to be away from glass. This was the first time we had bowed our heads to bombardment from the air. Not once during the long raids of 1940–1 had we left our apartment, and during February and March we only went down intermittently. But this time our nerves were slightly on edge and it seemed wiser to be sure of a good night in order to face more calmly the constant buzzing by day.

Our shelter was built of reinforced concrete, lit faintly by a shaded bulb. We arranged beds against the grey walls and looked rather like prisoners spending their final hours before being driven away to the execution block.

Bobby was delighted to find himself in this picturesque dormitory and, against all rules, brought Pouffy to sleep on the eiderdown. The atmosphere was oppressive and, however soundly we slept, we woke up tired the next morning. Our faintly lit dungeon gave us an extraordinary sense of safety—we slept as if drugged. In the old days dawn would have brought us relief. This time the start of a new day did not help matters in the slightest. We rose at eight, dishevelled, and climbed to the apartment, carrying the child, the pekinese and the blankets.

Breakfast was always important. We were hungry, glad to have come safely through the night and to find the apartment intact. We inspected the weather, hoping for some promise of sunshine. It was only six o'clock but there was never any glimpse of blue. Day after day heavy clouds and driving rain, leaden skies and a general atmosphere of damp gloom greeted us. What a month of June! What a contrast with that flaming summer of 1940 when Hitler was making *his* invasion! But it was good to have a bath and smell the coffee. Then as we began to live once more the sound would be heard, faintly at first and in the distance. This was the missile destined to fall amongst Londoners on their way to work. It came just after eight o'clock—sometimes there were two or three. They would fall, either by design or accident, between Victoria and Waterloo.

At a quarter past eight Myra, the housemaid, would arrive with the carpet-sweeper. She was tall and blonde, with a plaintive voice, and lived across the river in south London next door to our laundry, which had ceased to function because it had received a direct hit. Myra was an excellent girl. She looked after an aged but infirm mother and kept chickens, bringing an occasional egg for Bobby's breakfast. Her nights were far more disturbed than ours. The inhabitants of the suburbs were the real heroes of the flying bomb terror. But Myra, giving us the latest news of her district, never showed any sign of strain. She had a theory that she was immune from bombs.

As soon as she arrived the carpet-sweeper started to hum and life came to our great block of flats. Gradually we ceased to count the thuds and, crossing the park, my husband hardly looked up at the familiar sound but at the office, as work began, a dozen bells would start ringing furiously and people hurried down to the basement. Two or three minutes later there was a thud and more bells and everybody would run up again. Left alone in his office, he would telephone me, having a perverse determination not to follow the crowd. Only at the imminent danger signal would he leave the receiver dangling and run out into the passage to escape broken glass. And all the time it went on raining with a perseverance that was scarcely credible.

Disturbed nights and frequent alarms by day were not the only things to fray the nerves of office workers. Most young women had their husbands at the front in Normandy or with our armies in Italy. We began to hear of casualties being brought back by air from France. The experiences of two young women I knew were, I suspect, typical of what was going on all over town. One of them, who had last heard of her husband in the Cotentin, learned that he was in a London hospital suffering from shock. He ran into mortar fire while driving along a Normandy lane. His companion was killed outright. The top of his own crash helmet was blown clean off. Now the London sirens made him extremely nervous and the doctors decided to put him to sleep for five or six days to restore his nerves.

The other girl, who was also worried about her husband, received a telephone call at her office towards midday saying that her home in south London had been blown up a few moments earlier. Thus those who left their houses after a noisy night spent in an Anderson shelter never knew whether they would find their homes when they returned in the evening. The pilotless plane which just missed them at work might, for all they knew, fall on their loved ones. And meanwhile, they were anxious about their menfolk. All these things, together with the depressing weather, combined to produce a greater strain than during the Battle of Britain and, in fact, there was a good deal of cause for it.

By pure accident the next two bombs to fall in the heart of the town after the one on Sunday which destroyed the Guards Chapel at Wellington Barracks, were more or less in the same neighbourhood. One glided down on the garden wall of Buckingham Palace near Hyde Park Corner during the night; the other fell on some flats in Buckingham Gate, exactly opposite the barracks at about eight in the morning. The one that exploded on the garden wall of Buckingham Palace blew all the leaves off a splendid tree some yards away, making the branches bare as if in mid-winter. The amazing thing about this was that the boughs started to break out in bud again at the end of the autumn while other trees were losing their curled-up leaves.

When the weather cleared for a few moments one occasionally saw a bomb roaring overhead and one evening, while I was sitting in the Green Park, I watched a pilotless plane cut out and glide down over Covent Garden. There was an explosion and a spout of black smoke. Business in the theatre and restaurants started to decline and shopkeepers were hard hit because many people left town. We saw them leaving Carrington House in taxis piled with luggage. London was becoming once more the city of the brave and the few. Those of us who remained were learning to go about our business without taking much notice of the new terror.

The shopkeepers became more friendly. The customer was coming back into her own. One pilotless plane chose to skim our chimney pots during the lunch hour and everybody ran out to have a good look at it, which was not the wisest thing to do. The perils of the bomb affected people differently. One of our fishmongers, for instance, was intent on being able to say that he had seen one with his own eyes, whereas two of his customers decided to crouch under the slab on which he had been cutting the hake.

At about twenty-five minutes to one on the last day of June I was rounding Piccadilly Circus when, without any warning, a bomb fell at the back of the Regent Palace Hotel. None of us heard the engine. I was lifted up and deposited a few yards farther on as the blast roared in and out of the shops. Then the inevitable black smoke surged from the direction of Soho. At this time of the morning the Soho

The bombers' moon in the Green Park

Street market was in full swing, and there might have been many more casualties had the bomb dropped in the middle of it. As it happened, the damage was relatively small and was confined to the circus end of Brewer Street.

Except for one or two days when the sun seemed to shine by accident, July continued to bring us covered skies and a warm humidity, for ever suggesting rain. Our only consolation was to see the grass remain a tender green in our London parks when normally it would be turning yellow with the approach of August.

Mr Crouch, the suave head porter of Carrington House, who had a kind word for everybody, admitted that during his long hours of duty his thoughts were often with his family in the suburbs. The company had recently provided him with a new uniform, the upper half of which was a jacket instead of a knee-length coat, and though he had salvaged his silver buttons, he looked as if he had suddenly become an overgrown schoolboy. Had he been of less impressive stature, the dignity of his office might have been seriously impaired.

The pretty little Irish assistant at our baker's shop, whose young husband was killed in the R.A.F. only a few months after their marriage, seldom smiled and it was felt that she was often on the verge of tears. Does time heal these sorrows faster when one is only twenty? A young soldier, bewitched by her flashing Irish eyes, was so love-stricken that he dropped the loaf she handed him, fumbled with his change and, in short, was incapable of uttering a single word. When he had gone, I asked her if she felt able to start her life again. She smiled wistfully and answered: 'What's the good? He would only be killed like the other one.'

Bobby, in spite of our short holiday earlier in the year at Ross-on-Wye, seemed pale, and this was doubtless the result of sleeping every night in a cement blockhouse. On occasion, therefore, we risked spending the night in the apartment. What a pleasant change this proved! What a joy to stretch one's limbs between clean sheets—until one was wakened by the throbbing torpedo which filled the room with a rosy glow as it thundered above the housetops. Then I would dash to the cot with all the bedclothes ripped off the bed to throw over the sleeping child if the engine cut out. The horrible thing passed on only to be followed by another. When both had exploded at what for us was a safe distance I was overcome with the desire to seek once more that refreshing sleep that I was so much in need of. But now the flying bombs crept into my dreams. I woke up to find that the nightmare had translated itself into real life and that the room was illuminated once more with a red glow as the torpedo glided down on a town in which most of the inhabitants were hiding underground.

A new wave of Americans seemed to have arrived and they filled the streets. A small pony cart decorated with love-in-the-mist and marigolds passed through our market. Outside the beautiful Catholic church of Farm Street, where the King of Spain used to worship before the war, a bald, pugnacious-looking street vendor sold bunches of lavender, reproducing in stentorian tones the old eighteenth-century London street-cry. On Sunday morning it was quite usual for a flying bomb to land somewhere near a famous church in the West just after the service had started. This was doubt-less mere coincidence as London is dotted with famous churches. But we could almost set our clocks by it. The congregation at St George's, Hanover Square, where I was married, had a narrow escape when a flying bomb fell at the junction of Conduit Street and Regent Street. As it was so near us I went with Bobby to inspect the damage. I used to take him with me everywhere, and as he had grown up with this phenomenon he thought it perfectly normal to go on such expeditions, as children in Victorian times were taken to feast their eyes on the coloured balloons in Kensington Gardens. Strange had become the habits and amusements of Londoners. The war, though coming to an end, was far from being over. The R.A.F. had now abandoned the captive balloon site in the Green Park, leaving behind them not only the huts but also an excellent vegetable garden which the airmen had tended. As the girls had gone would it be dishonest to dig up the lettuces they had left behind? Mr Dijon, the chair man, had already left us. He had called on a colleague who was chef at a French service club and was invited to join the kitchen staff as pastrycook. Three weeks later he fell seriously ill. His wife who nursed him with great devotion died. This tragedy and his own illness left him looking a sick man and he had wasted all the summer. His hair was whiter and he only brightened up to show us a photograph of his son in uniform, adding that the boy had been transferred from Malta to the Italian front.

The number of women who formed our drawing-room coterie had increased; mine was the only child but most of us had dogs, and it was to exercise them, or at least to give them an outing, that most of the women had come there in the first place. Some lived at Arlington House, that beautiful block of apartments next to the Ritz and Wimborne House, others lived in Victoria and on the way to us crossed daily in front of Buckingham Palace, and one of them lived in a splendid apartment in Piccadilly. One afternoon, for instance, there came to sit beside me a woman wearing a cool dress and a hat of Italian straw of a quality no longer obtainable. We were under the lime trees and it was pleasantly warm. She said her name was Mrs Powys, and she was the wife of a London solicitor. In spite of five years of war, she still managed to be elegant, and I enjoyed her conversation which ranged over a variety of topics. She was essentially feminine and often described how, as a young unmarried woman before the war of 1914–18, her father sent her to spend a year in Paris with a very sedate French family. She moved there in a circle of French military and members of the Paris bar, who were all most enthusiastic about King Edward's entente cordiale. She amazed us by saying that soon after her arrival, a typical young English girl, she was severely reprimanded for crossing the road alone to post a letter—not only unchaperoned but without a hat! One of her chief ambitions as a girl was to travel on the top deck of a Paris horse-drawn bus which was then quite unthinkable for a young woman of quality. She did once achieve that ambition. She had gone with friends to visit the catacombs and afterwards persuaded a young man to take her home in a bus. At first he rebelled, pointing out that he was wearing a top hat and that it was not the thing for a young man in this attire to go on the top deck, but finally he agreed to do so on condition that he might remove his silk hat and carry it! The ascent was not easy for her. She was wearing a black straw hat with white wings, fixed to her head with a veil tied under the chin, and a long coat and narrow skirt, and she carried a tall parasol. She and her companion sat beside the good-natured Paris bus-driver, who spent the time telling them stories about the animals at the zoo. On her return she was once more scolded, and the following Sunday her hosts invited to lunch an elderly friend who had been told to give her a long lecture on the risks she had run in travelling on top of a bus.

One of her girlhood friends was Mme Picard, daughter-in-law of the Belgian Minister of Marine, who owned a hat shop, and it was in her workroom that the future Mrs Powys once made a hat for herself of pink linen with black straw, garnished with spotted net and tied under the chin with a black velvet ribbon. The slim-waisted Polaire, the popular French actress, seeing this hat in the shop, insisted on going off with it, leaving three golden louis which the English girl spent in giving a tea party to the *midinettes*.

Mrs Powys now had a daughter exactly the same age as she had been when living in Paris. Anne, her daughter, had no qualms about travelling on the top of a bus. She was a ferry pilot in the A.T.A. and her business was to deliver fighters and bombers from factory to airfield! But when I asked Anne if she thought her life was much more exciting than she pictured her mother's at the same age, she answered: 'I really don't think so. In mother's youth there were so

many things that a girl was supposed not to do that she
must have had a lot of fun doing them!'

Regimental bands still played in the Hyde Park bandstand
so that sitting under the trees one could recapture, in spite
of two wars, an Edwardian atmosphere. The Tommy took
his girl there to hold her by the hand, as his father did during
the war of 1914–18 and his grandfather when soldiers wore
red tunics and manly moustaches waxed at the ends.

Nevertheless a flying bomb fell less than a hundred yards
from where a nautical band was entertaining the public.
The following afternoon it played again as if nothing had
happened; indeed as I arrived with Bobby and Pouffy it
was just striking up 'Rule, Britannia' with suitable dash.
We sat beside a grey-haired American officer busily writing
a letter which I supposed was to his wife at home. The
fountain pen flew over the pad resting on his knees. His
thoughts continued thus far away through many other
rousing airs until, as a sign the concert had ended, the band
suddenly struck up 'God Save the King'. The American
officer was still so engrossed in his letter that for a moment
he seemed unaware of what was happening. Then he looked
up hurriedly, deposited his writing implements on an
adjoining chair, and rising self-consciously stood smartly
at the salute.

One of the oldest of the Hyde Park chair men, whom we
used to call Daisies because of his habit of referring thus
to his poor tired feet, bade me good-evening as the band
was dispersing, and added:

'Have you seen what the bomb did in the Dell, madam?'

He pointed to the lawn in front of what was known as the
Dell, this same lawn from which we had watched in the
autumn of 1940 the first German aerial armada setting fire
to the docks, a sight none of us who witnessed it would
forget. When, encouraged by Daisies, I reached this delightful spot I had the strange feeling of having brought my
small family out of summer into late autumn. Here was the

same phenomenon I had noticed in Kent when I saw my first flying bomb. Two proud catalpas, naked as in winter and both uprooted, were lying on the ground with their heads in opposite directions as if they had been wilted and brushed aside by the flaming breath of a dragon. There were two wizened pear trees and the upright trunk of a once stately chestnut. A weeping elm stood on the edge of the lawn with black arms twisted above its head like those of a contortionist—weeping, or rather, howling. I half expected to see the black arms winding and unwinding round the head of the tree as it continued its mournful dirge, but the strangest effect of this scene was the pungent odour which filled the air—the smell of sap from the trees stripped of their bark so that if you touched them they were wringing wet.

Meanwhile on the other side of the gravel path rabbits romped round the small, shallow lake in the Dell. Two Tommies and two Waafs were lying on the grass playing cards. What a strange contrast of life and death all this made! Cease to weep, unfortunate elm, I thought. By next spring your naked branches will be budding again. The gardeners say that it does you good to have your leaves lopped off from time to time and that afterwards you gain new vigour to give shade to courting couples in the park.

AUGUST, so packed with exciting news from France where two major fronts had by now developed, also brought the first real sunshine of the summer, but London had a sleepy, empty look and you could cross Bond Street at ten o'clock in the morning without seeing a single car. Holidays, the flying bombs and the fact that so many troops were over-seas contributed to this curious sensation of a city only half alive. Londoners were tired. They felt that the war was beginning to drag, and though the flying bombs had lost their first sting, enough slipped through the defences to make the suburbanites continue sleeping uncomfortably in their shelters. The others, those who lived in moderately safe buildings in the heart of London, crept back to their beds, but they also longed for a taste of sea air and a good invigorating breeze.

Yet here and there, almost for the first time since the war began, you could see a dash of bright paint in the street where somebody was able to liven up a door or a façade. People considered that the war was vitually finished and, though apprehensive of some new and more horrible secret weapon that might supersede the flying bomb, they looked inquiringly into the future, wondering what peace in Europe would bring.

Their interpretation of this question varied according to their age. Millie, the fashionable milliner in Berkeley Square, told me that a young duchess had sent her a box of pre-war Ascot hats with a note asking her to give them away to anybody who liked to adapt them for modern use, because after the war 'nobody will wear Ascot hats'. As Millie and her sister Kate lived in Carrington House, I had known them since the beginning of the war and I was always running round to the beautiful salon on the north side of that famous square in which, so the popular song said, nightingales sang. Tall, balconied windows opened on to the leafy trees and lush lawns in the centre of the square; in the salon the prettiest hats were displayed like roses of every colour at the end of long stems. Kate, who made the loveliest dresses, had a salon of her own on the floor above. The two sisters had a great affection for Bobby and Pouffy who would sit quietly in a corner while, rather like a spoilt daughter of the house, I tried on all the hats in turn. Millie's customers, besides the Queen who ordered little hats for Scotland and Mrs Winston Churchill who favoured snoods and scarves, consisted almost exclusively of the diplomatic corps and the peerage, and as she was the most delightful gossip I have ever known her conversation was positively scintillating. I was never rich enough to buy one of Millie's hats but she was so generous that she showered them upon

me. If I were to say to her: 'Millie I am going out to lunch
with So-and-so,' she would exclaim at once: 'But my dear,
you simply must wear a hat. I have the loveliest flowered
thing! You can bring it back to me on your way home and
tell me everything that happened at your lunch.' She read
the newspapers avidly and knew all the world figures
through their wives who came to her for a good gossip
while their husbands were busying themselves with the war.

Nothing ever ruffled Millie or Kate. Their professional
success was the sort of romance any girl would dream about.
One spring evening in 1915 Millie, then little more than a
girl, had gone to a *thé dansant* at the Piccadilly Hotel. She was
dressed, according to the fashion of the time, in a velvet
coat and skirt, and the skirt was ankle length and tight and
draped up the centre. After saying goodbye to her friend
in the foyer of the hotel, she decided to walk home to
Museum Street, where she then lived, by way of Shaftesbury
Avenue, but it happened that her coat and skirt had caught
the eyes of three other young women who were very anxious
to discover the name of her dressmaker. They followed
Millie as she picked her way through the crowded streets
and finally asked her for the all-important secret, but Millie
was obliged to admit that her only dressmaker was her
mother. 'Then,' said these young women, 'will you introduce us to your mother?' They were introduced and Millie's
mother made each of them a dress. These young women
became famous with the passing of time. Already they were
leaders of the fashionable world. One was Lady Diana
Manners, the second was Miss Iris Tree, daughter of Sir
Herbert Tree, the third Miss Jacqueline Alexander. They
brought their friends, and soon Millie's mother was unable
to cope with the work. Kate lent a hand, but her ideas
about dressmaking were not yet very professional. Her
clients would often have to help her cut the collar or the
sleeves. Then all of them would kneel on the floor with
scissors and material. One dress that fitted perfectly when
the client stood up burst all its seams when the client sat

down. But Kate must have been gifted, for when her mother died a year later, she carried on, and soon she was making dresses for many of the most fashionable women in Town. Millie made their hats. Strange indeed for Millie and her sister to be able to reflect upon the fashions of two wars and also upon the riotous years sandwiched in between. Shaw's play *Heartbreak House*, revived in the fourth year of the war, gave Londoners a gentle reminder of the fashions of 1917, and to many, I think, they must have brought back pictures of youth. These fashions were pleasing and ethereal and I, for one, would have loved to wear them.

Just after one o'clock on 23rd August I was walking along the dark and narrow alley called Whitehorse Street that leads from Piccadilly into Shepherd Market, when the sound of the 'Marseillaise' came from a radio in the American Club. If the B.B.C. had broken into their news broadcast to play the French national anthem, this was presumably to celebrate some specially important announcement. Passers-by stopped to listen. Yes, the news was indeed sensational. Paris was liberated.

One would have expected that Londoners would celebrate this tremendous victory but, whether it was that the capital was still relatively empty or that Londoners felt that it was not yet time to give vent to their emotions, they took the news philosophically. There was absolutely nothing in the streets to show that anything unusual had happened. However, it was announced later that the bells of both St Paul's and Westminster Abbey would ring out victory peals the following afternoon. But the next day Londoners continued to go about their business with that stoic look which made them suffer flying bombs and victories with equal resignation.

Soon after four o'clock, therefore, in the middle of a downpour, the bells of Westminster Abbey broke into their victory peal in honour of Notre Dame. The ringers did not know that, contrary to earlier reports, Paris was not yet entirely liberated, but the triumphant message echoed across the government offices of Whitehall where many civil servants were wondering if it was true that they might be moved to the country because of Germany's new secret weapon. If this really happened it would be a grim prelude to victory. For the women there was also a growing fear that when it was all over, they might be thrown out of their jobs to make way for the men.

These thoughts confused the message of the bellringers. At a few minutes after six the rain stopped, and I was just taking Bobby and Pouffy out for an airing when the sirens started to wail their warning to Londoners that another batch of flying bombs was hurtling through the low clouds.

The next morning news came that Paris was finally liberated. On this occasion London sparkled in brilliant sunshine.

AFTER the liberation of Paris came the liberation of Brussels, and then Londoners heard the grand news that the battle of the flying bomb was finished and that the lights of London were going up again. Thus it seemed that London was emerging at last from her trial—the fog and night of the long siege. The glow of lamps behind ordinary blinds would be seen for the first time since September 1939 when, at the beginning of the 'phoney' war, Londoners began to grope their way through medieval darkness.

One might have thought that a long-suffering public, burdened by five years of tiresome restrictions, extra duties, controls—in a word, all the uncomfortable vexations of war—would welcome with joyful enthusiasm the first signs of a gradual return to a more normal existence. What housewife, summoned from the kitchen by the peremptory ring of an angry warden complaining of a chink of light through her parlour window, had not returned to find the milk (so hard to come by) boiling over the gas-stove? Had we not heard all our middle-aged wage-earners complaining

about those exhausting Home Guard parades which sapped
their failing energy after a long day's work in the office?
Did they not grudge those Sundays when they had to
abandon the armchair, the warm fire, the well-worn manly
slippers and the joint to entrain for a route march through
sodden fields? And back at home at night, weary and caked
with mud, did they not beg a word of sympathy for rheu-
matic limbs and weak hearts?

Now a benevolent government lifted the black-out and
delivered the Home Guard from its compulsory parades.
What splendid news! Who minded it getting dark an hour
earlier? We could all walk through the streets of the town
admiring the soft glow from a thousand lightly curtained
windows, imagine our men in the Home Guard putting
away their uniforms, stretching their tired limbs and enjoying our company.

But we no sooner went out of doors than we discovered
that the black-out was as complete as ever and that there
was not a glimmer of light from any window. We would
bump against a man in khaki to find that he was a Home
Guard hurrying off to report for duty. Perhaps we made a
mistake and these rejoicings were for next week? No, the
Londoner was simply uncertain what to do with his liberty.
He is a creature of habit.

The fact was that long ago we doubled our chintz
curtains with black-out material to make sure that no
careless member of the family would get us into trouble,
and now it hardly seemed worth while to take them down
and unpick the lining. Besides, the chintz which was pink
or sky-blue when we bought it before the era of coupons
would need cleaning and we were waiting for spring. The
beginning of winter is no time to take down the trappings
of the house. Only a fortnight ago the laundry was destroyed
by a flying bomb; the French cleaners' also.

The Westminster City Council, it appeared, had also been
caught napping. Our streets would not be lighted for several
weeks yet. They were short of manpower and electric bulbs.

As for the Home Guard, he had reasons of his own for regretting the Government's decision to put his parades on a voluntary basis. For some time now the wife of a City man used to complain to her women friends in the Green Park drawing-room that her Home Guard was wearing himself out. But now, she said to us: 'He's broken-hearted! You see, he met men he would never have mixed with in peace-time—the local butcher, the fishmonger, the newsagent, not to mention a couple of influential bankers. They went through several tough nights during the raids and still like getting together one evening a week, and shooting at Bisley on Sundays. Now he will have to stay at home and take the dog out on Sunday mornings. The truth is that men like the company of other men. Yesterday, when one of them suggested they should meet for supper once a month just to keep up friendships and talk over old times, they collected £200 within a few minutes. I'm afraid I shall find him restless at home. And, frankly, his health has never been better.'

My other women friends rather echoed her sentiments. The very idea that the war might soon be over was ludicrously disturbing. Factory workers complained that they had passed the peak of their wartime earnings, and what would happen to the tradesmen who put all the good things under the counter? Others who had grumbled about the American invasion of London were shuddering at the thought that the boys from Wisconsin or Ohio might leave us. There were the shopkeepers who overcharged them, the street urchins who ran after them for chewing-gum and chocolate and most of all the female population who had learnt to appreciate flowers and candy and little compliments to keep us young. For once there had been more men than women in town. Anybody could guess that this desirable state of affairs could not last for ever.

Meanwhile our Government spokesmen, after celebrating the end of the flying-bomb season, made a series of eloquent speeches to prevent evacuees from returning to town. They claimed there was not enough milk to go round and that there was a shortage of accommodation, but they shouted to no avail, being unable to give the true reason— that whereas the V1 was practically finished, the V2 was just beginning.

This second secret weapon, this rocket projectile which hurtled down without warning from the stratosphere at a speed of over five hundred miles an hour, burying small houses in a neat crater some eighteen feet deep, rocking the whole town like an earthquake, became the major topic of conversation amongst Londoners who, unlike the Government, exchanged all the details in the market place. No sirens announced this new terror, which at first was mistaken for an explosion at an ammunition factory. Twin bangs sent unsuspecting victims to a speedy doom. At least there was none of that horrifying expectation which preceded the flying bomb as it rumbled over the housetops making straight towards you. The cellar was no longer at a premium—nor was the underground. The rocket dug its way deep into the ground, and for the first time one felt as safe on top of a building as at the bottom.

So all the evacuees who had come back to town now went off to the country again at the Government's expense.

THE Wellington Arch is that monumental affair at the Hyde Park Corner end of Constitution Hill. You will visualize it better if I tell you that it is surmounted by the winged chariot of peace, called the Quadriga, one of the best loved of London landmarks.

The arch is closed at its base by heavy wrought-iron gates, which are flung open when royalty drives from Buckingham Palace to Hyde Park Corner. This is the route our monarchs take when driving, for instance, to Windsor Castle. The royal limousine, instead of going round Hyde Park Corner which is a traffic roundabout, cuts straight across the circle. During the autumn of 1944 the private carriageway had on one side of it a mound of earth thrown up from Hyde Park when trenches were dug there during the Munich crisis. Londoners were surprised to notice that it gradually became covered with alpine plants.

The base of Wellington Arch concealed a small and little known police station, and the men stationed here were as tall as guardsmen and nicknamed 'Park statues' or 'Six-foot Freddie Bartholomews'. They dealt with royalty and went where royalty went. The father of one of these men happened to be a nurseryman and as he specialized in 'alpines', the son used to go out at midnight and plant some of the rarest specimens in his father's collection opposite the police station.

On the one occasion when I went there the sirens had been silent all day. One of the tall, good-looking police constables of A Division had offered to show me round. The station office to my surprise was a perfect Victorian period piece and was about as large as a set on a West End stage. As soon as one stepped inside one pictured a London of dense winter fogs, antimacassars and hansom cabs. It was low-ceilinged and heavily pillared. A century-old octagonal rosewood clock with 'M.P.' on either side of the crown bore witness that it was made by John Meader of Albany Street, Regent's Park, only four years after a youthful Queen Victoria had mounted the throne. A heavy desk with an armchair as impressive as any sat upon by a High Court judge, an open fire above which hung the giant key to open the iron gates, all sorts of mysterious shadows in the semi-darkness behind the pillars, and a hurricane lamp suspended from the ochre-domed ceiling—all this was charmingly period.

Mysterious were the steep staircases and half-empty rooms which formed the rest of the castle. There were some eighty steps to the loft, which must once have been a blacksmith's shop; and a dozen more to the balustrade running round the massive winged chariot. What a fine view from the balustrade, especially on this autumn evening when the

sun was setting over Knightsbridge, painting the sky
crimson.

I stood there for a long time with my six-foot-tall companion looking down on the sparse traffic below. From this
height one saw St George's Hospital looking like a super-
imposed settlement. The police of Wellington Arch knew
every inch of that hospital, for they had taken many a
casualty there.

What a study in colonnades was the architecture there-
about—the columns of the hospital, the Ionic pillars of the
Duke of Wellington's mansion with its flagpole knocked
askew by the bomb which sliced out a couple of houses from
the aristocratic row in which King George VI and Queen
Elizabeth lived when they were Duke and Duchess of
York. We were so high that the trees of the Green Park,
those on either side of Constitution Hill and those in the
gardens of Buckingham Palace—London plane trees mostly
and still in full leaf—made a veritable ocean of green, the
surface of which, as I looked down on it, was rippled by the
breeze. Distant landmarks—all but the tower of Westminster Cathedral and that of Big Ben—were lost in the
evening mist. Two herons flapped their way just above our
heads, flying from Hyde Park to the lake in St James's
Park. The moon was rising above the palace, filling the
sky with a milkiness that was in ghostly contrast to the
orange glow of the setting sun in the west. The trees which
three months earlier lost all their foliage when two flying
bombs crashed within a few feet of each other just inside
the railings of the gardens of Buckingham Palace, were
now green again—remarkable proof that nature triumphs
over everything and can make a tree burst into bud as
easily in September as in the spring.

'The sirens that have warned you of every air raid during
the last four years', said the constable, 'are at your feet
between the wheels of the chariot. If they were to sound now,
don't be frightened. All you need do is to put your hands
to your ears.'

I stepped back involuntarily.

'Oh,' he said, 'it's not as bad as all that. We even kept rabbits here for a time and they played under the shadow of this peace symbol all through the battle of London. Neither flak nor searchlights worried them.'

I walked home across the Green Park to see if there were any of my friends on our favourite lawn between the five Cornish elms and the sump. A young married woman was telling the others about her mother-in-law's stratagem for transporting herself and five trunks to a friend's country house fifty miles from London. The old lady, who was over seventy, could never be prevailed upon to travel light. In her Edwardian youth she had been brought up to do things on a grand scale. She would, for instance, take several trunks with her—one for her hats, one for her shoes, one for her dresses, and so on, and her maid would travel ahead with them.

When, therefore, some weeks earlier she had received an invitation from a lifelong friend to spend a month in her country house she had insisted on packing at least two or three trunks. However, she no longer had a maid and the railway company was unco-operative about the luggage. There were other difficulties such as the lack of porters (even if she did travel by rail) and the uncertainty of finding a taxi at the other end. Being resourceful she solved these problems by hiring a removal van.

When the van arrived at her London place to collect the luggage she added a kitchen chair for her own use, and in this way made the journey to her friend.

Her hosts received her affectionately but, as they had no more servants to run a house where there were usually a dozen, the old lady gladly lent a hand. She swept her room, made her bed and offered each morning to feed thirty-two rabbits. Before the end of the month, however, the old lady decided that even country air did not compensate for living in an unheated mansion, so she 'removed' herself back to

Flying bombs in Highfield, Kent, by Lady Cohen

A rainy day during the battle of the flying bombs

Crewe House

Duck Island Cottage, S.W.

London. When the van drove up to the historic mansion, everybody turned out to watch the old lady seat herself on the kitchen chair. The driver asked: 'Where to?'

'I would like to go to the International Sporting Club in Park Lane,' said the old lady.

'Very well, ma'am.'

'But my dear,' said her hostess, 'what *will* they think?'

When, after quite a comfortable journey, the van drew up in Park Lane, the commissionaire, who had known her for many years, she being a founder-member, showed no surprise.

'I do hope', said the old lady, 'that you are not shocked to see me arrive in a furniture van?'

'Certainly not, madam,' he answered. 'Why, only this morning Lady X arrived at the club in a milk-float.'

TOWARDS the middle of October I paid a second visit to Highfield. Autumn daisies had replaced the roses of June, and apples and pears were now being stored on wide trays in the outhouses. The beech trees were changing colour and the lawns were strewn with curly brown leaves, making a rustling carpet over the grass that was still green. But the most important change of all was that the battle of the flying bomb, which we had seen in its initial stage during our first visit, was now ended, and the only sound in the sky on this beautiful autumnal day was the steady roar of heavy bombers winding their way like silver arrows towards the heart of the Rhineland to join in the struggle for Aachen.

A complete stranger who drove us up from the station (purely out of kindness) said that no fewer than thirty-six people were killed in and around the village during the last months. The great balloon barrage which stretched across the inland downs formed one of the rungs in the outer defences of London. People prayed that these ugly missiles would fall on their fair fields rather than on the built-up areas of the capital. But there were times when they came so close that in the words of Sir Herbert: 'Our first reaction was one of fear for those about us. But as soon as the bomb passed, we felt ashamed of our selfishness, knowing that in two and a half minutes we should hear the thud as it exploded in London.'

As soon as I entered the drawing-room with Bobby I saw, leaning against a chair, the canvas of a painting our hostess had made from the bottom of the garden. It showed one of the many balloons on the estate—this particular one resting on the cricket field where so often her two sons (both killed) had played. The sky was filled with these silver ships riding at anchor, making a dense curtain, and in the picture they looked like dabs of cotton-wool. The young R.A.F. boys looking after these balloons received from their hosts much of the affection that, alas, could no longer be bestowed on the soldier sons. Lord Dunsany wrote of Stephen:

> The land he loved will be
> Still the old land he knew,
> And though he will not see
> Bright April coming through,
> The hazels with the blue
> Of hyacinths, and glee
> Of birds, when every tree
> Rings with their melody,
> He has done all he could
> That valley, hill and wood,
> High down and Darenth stream
> See not, through smoke and blood,
> The hell of Hitler's dream.

On my return to London I found that William Hayward, who used to preside over the five or six little shops bearing his father's name which were dotted about Shepherd Market, had retired to the country, and though the family (William's father was over ninety) retained an interest in them, a manager was appointed to the grocery store in the

main street. The façade of this public meeting-place had
recently been painted green, and the windows, which had
been boarded up since the great fire in the market during
the big raid in the spring of 1941, were now glazed and
polished. In every way, therefore, Hayward's grocery shop
became as gay, as busy and as picturesque as it had ever
been.

The new manager was seventy. He was tall, broad-
shouldered, with deep-set eyes and a strong voice, and he
had a general resemblance to Chaliapin, which was made
even more striking by the tuft of grey-white hair which rose
majestically above his high forehead. His name was John
Robert Richens. For quite a long time I paid no special
attention to him except for remarking on his likeness to the
great Russian singer, but one misty October morning, while
waiting with some other women to be served, I witnessed by
accident one of those little dramas which suddenly put
familiar faces in a different light, clothing them with adventure or tragedy.

In front of me was a slightly built, elderly woman in
black with a three-cornered marquis hat over beautiful
white hair decorated at the back by a tiny bow of black
velvet. This little lady carried herself with aristocratic
bearing, holding her shopping bag not at her side but in
front of her, and I noticed in particular her lorgnette and the
white pearls round her neck.

'Good morning, Richens,' she said. 'Have you any news?'

'Alas, no, Mrs La Mottee,' he answered, 'and have
you?'

'No, indeed,' she said sadly. 'I am afraid it will be some
time yet.'

All the rest of the day this small incident kept running
through my head, and in the evening, seeing Mr Richens
standing in the doorway of the shop, his frame slightly
bent but his fine head thrown up as if ready to burst into
song, I said to him:

'Mr Richens, who was the lady you were speaking to this

morning, and what is the news you appear to be both so eager for?'

He looked down and almost gruffly answered:

'Mrs La Mottee? Who is Mrs La Mottee? Why, Mrs La Mottee is what we used to call a member of the Gentry of the Island, or, if you prefer it, one of the Upper Ten.'

'But of what island?'

'Guernsey, of course, where I owned a grocery shop which I built up to be the finest privately owned retail business in the island. Mrs La Mottee lived two doors away from Victor Hugo's house and she was a regular customer of mine. Though, in a sense, we are both refugees, fate has thrown us together again, and she continues to be my customer, while I continue to have the honour of serving her.'

So it was news of Guernsey that they were both so anxious to have.

Though Mr Richens was not exactly talkative, it was not long before I was able to piece together his story. He told it by degrees between serving his customers with two ounces of butter, and cutting up our ration books with a long pair of scissors, while his unrimmed spectacles were pushed up on his noble forehead.

John Robert Richens, of Huguenot descent, was born in a Berkshire village where all his people were farmers. He was sent to Oxford to learn the grocery trade and, at the age of twenty, came up to London where he worked in Eastcheap, but his health was weak and the doctor advised him to go to the Channel Islands. After spending a few weeks in Jersey, he moved to Guernsey and started as an assistant at the grocery store he was later to own. 'My son was only three when I took the business over,' he said. 'The lad is now thirty-seven.'

So he worked the business up until it became not only a retail but a wholesale firm—twenty employees, three lorries and two light cars. Then, as the first Germans were pushing off from Cherbourg to occupy the island, Richens, with his family, escaped in a tanker carrying eighty thousand gallons of aviation spirit, and for two years, almost a stranger in London, he was ill and hardly able to earn a living.

I therefore saw this brave septuagenarian in a new light, and like Mrs La Mottee, I took to asking him if he had received any news, but the answer was always the same, and the once-rich trader, having become (too late in life) a modest employee, went on cutting up ration books and little slabs of butter. Between Mrs La Mottee and myself also grew up an understanding, and the day came when she invited Bobby and me to tea at her brother's house in Hertford Street where she had gone to live.

Hertford Street was by then a ruin of its old self.

From that part of it which was at right angles to Carrington House, as far as Londonderry House at the corner of Park Lane, every other house was either grim and blasted, or turned into billets for British or American troops. In one, the Royal Corps of Signals kept their carrier pigeons and a wireless set that blared out canned music; another was turned into an Irish Club. The street was noisy and sad; the façades unkempt and unpainted. But there was one exception which you might never have noticed had you not been looking for it. The number was thirty-four, and it was built by Willett, the builder (and originator of summer time), some forty years earlier for his own use, and was now owned by Mrs La Mottee's brother, General Sir Beauvoir de Lisle. To this house, therefore, I took my child to tea.

I had expected—well, in truth, I hardly know what I had expected, but certainly not such a trim little house full of eighteenth-century furniture, pleasantly lighted pictures, and Waterford glass and Spode china in cases against the walls. How could these fragile objects have lived through the bombardments when the public-house just behind was in ruins, and every window in the neighbourhood had been smashed? The general was just as trim as his home, just as unruffled, with a gentle, old-world courtesy, and a way of letting you know that he had no intention of allowing the war to interfere with his exquisite manners or the way he decorated his house. His sister was even more dignified in this setting than in the market doing her shopping. She was, as usual, dressed in black, with the pearls round her neck and the little bow at the back of her snow-white hair. She moved with easy grace through the wide hall in the middle of which tea was laid on a long oak table.

'Beau', she said to me, speaking of her brother, 'slept quietly in his bed through every one of the raids except for that memorable occasion when he was blown out of it and had to finish the night in the drawing-room. And what is more, he dresses for dinner every evening—yes, every single evening, just as he did at Poona.'

'Bombs,' put in the general. 'They either kill you or leave you alone. There's no use worrying about them. You don't like bombs, madam?'

'No,' I answered truthfully. 'I do not. Your philosophy is all very well but I can't help thinking about flying glass.'

'Yes, there is glass,' answered the general somewhat against his will, 'but neither a plate nor a piece of glass [he was thinking of his Waterford], other than a few windows, was ever broken in this house. What will you? The walls are strong—concrete and steel—old Willett knew his business.'

We sat down, and the general poured out the tea from a silver teapot polished by himself. I looked at Mrs La Mottee at the other end of the table and wondered what her house was like in Guernsey. I told her that Mr Richens had described her as a member of the Upper Ten, and added that, by the strangest coincidence, I had just been reading a life of Victor Hugo by Léon Daudet, which made me specially interested in the poet's house on the island.

'My cat had a way of wandering into the garden of Victor Hugo's house which is now a museum,' she answered. 'I never thought much of the house (it is true that Victor Hugo had a strange taste in furniture), but I knew the garden

well because I was always going into it to retrieve my cat.'
Mrs La Mottee added: 'We had the most lovely view across
the bay, and in fine weather, through glasses, we could see
the lighthouse at Cherbourg. This was the view the exiled
French poet looked upon from his glass look-out when
writing *Les Misérables*.'

However much the exiled Mrs La Mottee may have been
thinking about her house, she appeared more immediately
concerned about the fact that her only maid was leaving
her to get married that same day, and she wondered if her
brother would be satisfied with her cooking. 'It's hard at
my age', she said, 'to start doing things one has never done
before.'

But the general said:

'I clean the front steps and the brass. The other day a
passing taxi-driver called out: "Times have changed, sir."
And only last week,' the general continued, 'I saw my old
friend Field Marshal Lord Milne (we were at Staff College
together) walking down Hertford Street, and I said to him:
"How's the world treating you?" to which he answered:
"Oh, I'm like everybody else. My wife cooks, and I do the
washing-up."'

The general had a sentimental affection for this part of
London, which he was gradually instilling into his sister
to prevent her from thinking too much about Guernsey.
He had a gift for recalling the past glories of Curzon Street
and Berkeley Square before the advent of steel and cement.
As he talked, one pictured the people who lived in the big
comfortable houses surrounded by large leafy gardens. He
made me feel almost at home with old Lansdowne House,
whose owner in the eighties he had met in India when he
was a younger man and the marquis was viceroy. After
their return to England, Lansdowne told the younger man
how the game of lawn tennis was born in the gardens of his
mansion in Berkeley Square. The thing happened in the
summer of 1869. A young captain of artillery called Major
Wingfield drove up to Berkeley Square to tell Lord Lans-

downe that he had just invented a new game that four players could learn on a nicely mown lawn. The noble peer was interested and told the major to come to tea the following day, when he would invite Walter Long and Arthur Balfour to make up the requisite number.

And so the first game of lawn tennis was played in that garden overlooking Berkeley Square, a fact which to my mind is even more romantic than the myth about the nightingale. The general added that the game was played over a net about two feet tall, hung from sloping posts kept up by strings attached to pegs. The four players met several times a week to play the game and draw up the rules, and it was Arthur Balfour who named it lawn tennis. This was the Arthur Balfour who later became Prime Minister.

Incidentally the flying bomb that gave us such a shaking in the summer, landed exactly where the four men played their first game of lawn tennis in the sixties.

In prints of old London Bridge one sees it crowned with quaint houses under which the water swirled down to the sea. Until the great fire of 1940 which destroyed so much of Shepherd Market there were two picturesque passageways surmounted by Georgian houses dividing the market from Curzon Street. One of these passageways was still there to remind us of the quaintness of bygone times.

Approaching Curzon Street by way of this passage, I passed almost every day the baker on the left and a fruiterer on the right. These two establishments were bridged on the level of the first floor by the dining-room of the Colonial Club with its tall, narrow windows, bright with chintz curtains and pretty flowers.

To this part of the world, some fifteen years earlier, had come a slip of a girl called Eileen Parsons, who figured in the newspapers when she was bequeathed five hundred pounds in recognition of her fortitude during the battle of London by the late Mr Frank Jefferys, the proprietor of the baker's shop which never failed to bake its crisp loaves and golden rolls in spite of high explosives and fire bombs.

Two years after the death of Mr Frank Jefferys, his widow went to live in the country, and the bakery passed into other hands, but Eileen, with her brown hair and finely chiselled features, was still behind the counter, and I would buy my hot loaves from her within a few minutes of their leaving the oven.

Our village was still, in spite of the bombs, a stronghold of little artisans. The oldest oven in the bakery had been built over a century earlier by a firm in Leicester Square which had long ago ceased to exist. Bread was baked three times a day, and the village cats were well aware of this peculiarity, for on cold days one found them contentedly snoozing on the pavement in Curzon Street which was immediately above the pastrycook's five-bushel oven.

John Wilmore, the pastrycook, covered from head to feet in white flour, worked like Mephistopheles in the sinister red glare of his oven, the roof of which quivered under the weight of passing taxis and jeeps. He wielded with astonishing skill his 'peel' of American ash, an instrument with a very long handle like that of a billiard cue, but which was flat and circular at the end like a ping-pong racket. With this he prised up his chocolate-flavoured cakes and brought them out all hot and brown.

John Wilmore was a foreman without a staff (his men having been called up), and the only living creature to watch every movement of his supple arms was Peter the tabby cat, who had royal blood, having been born within the precincts of Buckingham Palace of a sleek and beautiful favourite of the King and Queen. John and the royal cat were masters of a realm which was all snowy white with pre-war Canadian flour, lately released by the Ministry of Food, and on all this the furnace cast a red glow like a sinking sun on a northern landscape. John was a Londoner wise in London lore, and remembered the pre-1914 days when Mr Mason and his two sons, for whom he worked in

Sloane Street, came to that aristocratically Edwardian tea-shop every morning in frock-coat, top-hat, and lavender trousers strapped under the instep.

The bread was baked on the first floor, level with the bridge, and George Duffield, the baker, wore a flat white toque like a linen beret, and his drooping moustaches in their natural state were jet black. The rolls and French loaves, freshly kneaded and still white and elastic, came down in large wooden trays, and as soon as the oven was right, Duffield and his mate placed two dozen or more on the 'slip' (brother to the 'peel' and made like an elongated wooden paper-knife), lifted up the oven door, and jerked them in neat rows with a flip of the wrist. Down came the door again, and the 'slip' was sprayed with flour, more rolls and French loaves were laid along it, and the process started again.

How good it all smelt! I remembered arriving at a tiny Swiss village one spring morning when it was still dark, to hear the tinkle of cowbells on the mountainside and to smell the baking bread which, in the clear, crystal air, mingled with the scent of wild thyme, marguerites and charcoal.

Our village had no wild thyme or marguerites and we relied for our flowers on Miss Bunbury, one of whose ancestors was made so famous by Sir Joshua Reynolds. She came up every morning with the bouquets she had cut before breakfast in her country home.

Wilmore and Duffield were justly proud of having carried on right through the battle of London, baking their bread and their cakes while the bombs fell, even refusing to give up when a high explosive hit the gas main, so that they were obliged to spend the whole morning converting their ovens from gas to coal. Our market had been without gas for ten days. Then Duffield cooked the joints for our villagers in his bread oven. Those anxious days and nights doubtless hastened poor Frank Jefferys to his grave. I almost ran into his coffin the day of the funeral as I was hurrying into the shop, for I knew nothing of the tragedy until I saw the bier being carried out, followed by the staff. Here also I nearly lost my baby in his pram. The huge plate-glass windows of the bakery crashed into the street where less than half a minute earlier I had left the child, the dog and my shopping in the pram! The sneak raider (there had been no alarm) zoomed above the chimney pots and was out of sight before the sirens went. Less than half a minute and Bobby would have joined the victims laid out on the cold floor of the bar in 'Dirty Dick's'! This was my worst moment in the whole war.

On 11th November I took Bobby and Pouffy shopping in Soho. The sky was overcast and the pavements were doing their best to dry between showers. The shops were filled with apples and chrysanthemums and onions, and it seemed curious to reflect that only a few years earlier onions were so rare that people made jokes about them, and they were put up for auction in charity sales. The chrysanthemums were not at their best; they had been touched by the frost, and in this semi-continental setting were evocative of All Saints' Day and funeral wreaths. The apples were splendid and abundant—green cooking apples, russets and Cox's orange pippins, and they were reasonably cheap because price was controlled.

This was the sixth time during the war that we were celebrating the end of the previous one. Most of the American G.I.s who infiltrated into Soho from the Rainbow Club at the top of Shaftesbury Avenue, where they kicked their heels and smoked cigars on the pavement, were not even born when the world went mad in November 1918. But they all bought poppies and some of them bought two as if they were delighted to find something on which to spend their money. The poppies were all that remained of the sad November pageantry which even during the last years of peace had been gradually diminishing. The vast crowds at the Cenotaph, King George V, the Prince of Wales, the hushed silence and bared heads . . . these were rather painful memories, as if we were ashamed that we had allowed it all to be in vain.

From time to time, walking five or six abreast, came some Tommies wearing red ties, blue trousers, and khaki caps. Some of them hobbled on new crutches, others had an arm in a sling. One of the most curious things of the last few months was the comparative rarity of the British Tommy in the streets of London. These were the wounded from the Normandy beach-head—the June invasion of the continent —strong enough now to leave hospital for a few hours a day. They walked silently, slowly, apathetically, taking up half the width of Old Compton Street, and one was obliged to take notice of them, and the sight of them gave one a little lump in the throat. Nobody, however, ran out of the shops to welcome them, to pat them on the back, or to offer them cigarettes. There was none of the effusion of the last war. They also wore poppies in their button-holes. Women with shopping baskets looked at them, appeared to hesitate a moment, and then hurried off to buy a pound of tomatoes which, by now, were beginning to be scarce. They seemed aggrieved that the war was still on. So many people had prophesied that it would be over in Europe by Armistice Day.

ALL my friends of the cross-channel steamer were now dispersed. The intrepid Pierre, so long a figure of romance and mystery, was dead. The days of perilous trips to the Continent were over. No longer were brave agents obliged to crop their hair, disguise their features and parachute themselves on dark nights over the fields of France or Belgium. We did not gather like conspirators to admire a bunch of wild flowers gathered surreptitiously on some desolate strip of the Picardy coast by a courier on his way back to England from a dangerous mission. We didn't speak in hushed tones of Paris or Brussels as if they were a million miles away. British and American planes roared over there in less than an hour with diplomats, Allied officers and newspaper correspondents.

The Lady of Paris had returned to the French capital shortly after its liberation. She occupied an important post in her country's administration, spoke on the radio, and carried forward to some extent her husband's political career. One of the main streets in Paris was given her husband's name and the newspapers printed photographs of his widow (her arms filled with flowers) at the opening ceremony. Young Anne Brossolette, the daughter, who had been sent to Sherborne to learn the English way of life, wrote from Dorset that she was enjoying every moment of it. The great school enchanted her. Charles, our Belgian friend, had resumed his journalistic career. His book on the Spanish prison camps, on which he worked so assiduously during his two years' stay in London, had been published. Anne Hellequin, the Angel of Brittany, was still in London. Occasionally, as one passed along Piccadilly, one would see a low covered truck drawn up beside the Berkeley Hotel from which emerged two or three important-looking men, gripping bulky valises from which fluttered labels with the words 'Passenger from Brussels' or 'Passenger from Paris'.

Meanwhile Christmas was only three weeks distant. There was nothing in the shops particularly to remind one that this was so, but it was already in the air and Piccadilly at lunch time had that effervescence which is unmistakable. Occasionally, once or twice, sometimes more often in the twenty-four hours, one heard that crunching, rumbling sound, that uncomfortable tremor, which signalled the explosion of a V2. So far there had not been many in the heart of London—the nearest, I fancy, was in Holborn—but one of these missiles plunged into the mud of the Thames almost opposite the Savoy Hotel, shattering for the seventh time the huge windows of the famous restaurant facing the Victoria Embankment.

The mud-banks of the Thames between the bridges of Charing Cross and Blackfriars had already received several tons of high explosives of various kinds which might otherwise have done widespread damage. During the summer a V1 dived into the river opposite the Adelphi, spraying Charing Cross Bridge and blasting windows as far as the Strand. To some extent, therefore, the river played the same role as our London parks, taking the shock of many a bomb.

The news that the Thames (at such a famous bend of its course) had swallowed up a V2 was sufficiently known by the Monday morning for people to peer over the Embankment to discover exactly where it dropped. Imagine the perfect winter day—a blue sky, a big flaming sun above the County Hall, and a cold, dry wind which made ripples on the water. The sun, not hot enough to give one any appreciable warmth, was bright enough to give a sparkle to all the tall buildings stretching majestically from the Adelphi to Somerset House. How this skyline shimmered in the clear air, its mighty façades disdainful of the cardboard and linen flapping from blasted window casings! These gleaming edifices were nearly as white as the new Waterloo Bridge gracefully spanning the river and only just completely opened to traffic. The dazzle of clean stone made Cleopatra's Needle look pathetically black. The Egyptian treasure, corroded by more than half a century of London grime and fog, this delicate prisoner from a hot climate, was consumptive, pining for the burning desert. A train rolled over Charing Cross Bridge and the noise of the heavy coaches and the sight of the smoke belching from the engine reminded one of the nostalgia of Kipling's 'go-fever' hero, Dick, in *The Light that Failed*, and somehow one coupled this up with Bessie's question, 'Where is the desert?' and Dick's answer: 'East—out of the mouth of the river. Then west, then south, and then east again, all along the underside of Europe. Then south again, God knows how far.' If Cleopatra's Needle had a soul, it must occasionally have tried to fly in that direction.

Leaning against the Embankment parapet, an old man

with a pitted red face was pointing with a short clay pipe, the bowl turned downwards, in the direction of the mud flats of the opposite shore. He claimed to know just where the V2 fell, and was anxious to impart his knowledge to a small but interested audience.

'See where them pebbles are,' he said. 'Thrown up by the explosion, they was. The mud's littered with 'em.' Then, turning to me: 'Not there, lady. Further along—the other side of the new bridge. Beyond the dredger wot's pulling up the foundations of the old 'un.' Finally to his audience as a whole: 'Like quicksands, that mud. There was a big 'ole there yesterday. Today there's only the pebbles left. Queer, ain't it?'

I walked as far as the Savoy, past Brettenham House and the Institute of Electrical Engineers where workmen were mending the windows, to lunch with a friend just back from America who seemed to think that in New York there were too many cocktail parties, too much gaiety, too many signs of prosperity—but I could not help thinking of the G.I.s in my own part of London and how they were beginning to be liked and to feel genuinely at home. To Curzon Street, for instance, they were themselves bringing customs and pictures reminiscent of 42nd Street. I liked the blending of the two continents. I liked those two London partners who worked early and late in their tailors' shop opposite the Washington Club ironing American uniforms, sewing on buttons, mending, taking out stains, pressing greatcoats and what the Yankees called 'blouses' and 'pinks'. I was not the only one to find glamour in Whitehorse Street, where the kitchens of the In and Out Club and those of the American Club sent up through windows their appetizing odours, where half the narrow street was lined with jeeps, and where London costers came to sell their wares.

SOME people said that the V2s were quietly finding their

range. Four nights later, on the 6th December to be exact, while I was reading a book by Mrs Gaskell, Carrington House shook so vigorously that a door slammed, and Bobby cried out in his cot. Having been jerked back with great speed from the moors of Yorkshire to the battlefield of Mayfair, I prepared with rather a sick heart to retire for the night, and it was only the next morning, when calling at Andrey's paper shop, that I was told that the thing had crashed on a public-house near the eastern wing of Selfridge's. When later I passed that way I found that many of the fir trees which with coloured lights had festooned the whole length of the famous store were now strewn on the pavement. Tinsel was being swept into the gutters. Such a dismal picture would have needed the genius of Hans Andersen.

Extraordinary was the excitement that this bomb caused, partly because it was the first of its kind to do great damage in the West End, partly from a feeling of rage that, after mastering its predecessor the V1, after pushing the Germans back to their frontiers, after dismissing the Home Guard and partially lifting the black-out, after hearing our politicians telling us that the bomb menace was virtually at an end, and after resigning ourselves to another Christmas at war, we should be plagued by these meteors which were now likely to increase rather than to diminish.

There was a trail of broken glass along Oxford Street, down Orchard Street and half way up Wigmore Street. The shopping crowds were not any smaller because of what the authorities called a major incident. Many women, less well informed than myself who lived so near, must have fallen upon it unawares. The shop girls were surprised as soon as they clocked in to be given brushes and pans and told to clean up the debris in their department. But in the street there was nothing new. We had seen it everywhere during the raids of 1940–1 and again during the February–March raids of this year, and during the devastating battle of the flying bombs. The chief difference was in the speed and

Shepherd Market: Oscar's public house

The air-raid siren at the Wellington Arch

mechanization of rescue and repair work which was going on behind the barriers. The American squads, organized and supplied on military lines, applied the large-scale American technique to the job.

Londoners could no longer wander amongst the wreckage as they could in the early days of the war. The public was kept to the outer perimeter, which was a good thing because many women, as I had done, insisted on wheeling their prams while shopkeepers shovelled out glass from upper windows. While people were surging round the cordon, gaping at the strange tricks of blast and crowding into shops, men of the heavy rescue squad were digging for bodies under the wreckage inside the cordon, and half a dozen members of the Women's Voluntary Service, wearing their green overcoats and berets, were, by close and sympathetic interrogation, disentangling the tragedies of the night at their post in the classroom of a girls' school, the windows of which were all broken.

They sat, these women, at a deal table against the wall at the far end of the room, and because it was bitterly cold most of them had rugs round their knees. I drew up a chair and sat beside them, listening to the stories of all the poor folk who, with drawn faces and clothes grimed with dust and minute particles of plaster, had come to inquire about relatives or neighbours, injured, dead or missing.

In this classroom there were six rows of little desks facing a long blackboard on which remained traces of the last lesson, the subject of which was geography. The mistress had written in a clear hand figures appertaining to the area and population of the United Kingdom. On a smaller blackboard, stacked against an easel beside the window where the glaziers were already putting in new glass, some little girl had drawn a circle with two eyes, a nose, and a mouth, above which she had written: 'Teacher.'

What a bright place this must have been! The octagonal clock was still ticking above the larger of the blackboards, and a red sun, piercing the morning mist, was comforting us. Round the walls of the classroom were square tiles depicting the birds and animals on a farm—goats and, against white clouds, geese, hens, shire horses, and here and there some Dutch windmills. The harmonium, up against the windows, was covered by brown paper, and glaziers were using this as a table on which to mix putty. Now from the hall came shrill, clear voices that momentarily drowned the low mumbling of an old woman clasping an injured cat to her breast as she told her story haltingly to the woman next to me. The interruption came from a handful of little girls who were being told by their mistress that there would be no lessons today. The woman with the cat was now explaining how she had lost her one-room home, for which she paid one pound a week. When told that it would be made fit to live in again, she burst into tears of gratitude. She was asked if she would like a cup of tea, but though she had been without sustenance since the previous night, she refused, saying that she only drank or ate at regular hours. My neighbour then explained that until her room was repaired she would have to lodge elsewhere, and that there was a hostel willing to give her food and shelter but that the rules forbade its guests to keep animals. At this point some charitable person suggested that arrangements could be made for the tabby to put painlessly to sleep, but on hearing this the old lady again burst into tears, not tears of gratitude this time, but the most heartbreaking flood of helpless alarm, as if life was not worth thinking of without a cat, and so it was settled that one of the wardens would build a small cupboard in the damaged flat where the cat would live, and that every day the old lady would come to give it food and exercise.

It was just this infinite attention to detail that made the work of the W.V.S. so admirable, for most of these helpers had children of their own to look after, meals to prepare at home, housework and shopping, and it was no small sacrifice to take their rota of rescue duty, comforting the distressed and bracing up their own courage to drive the

dead to the mortuary. In addition to all this, some of the
women had full-time professions. Beryl Hearnden, for instance, a writer of detective stories, was now engaged
on real-life problems vital and pathetic. I found her trying
to puzzle out to whom belonged some torn sheets of a ration
card found in the little girls' classroom. Could it be true, as
one of the mistresses had told her, that two women had
been scalped by the explosion and that rescue workers had
picked up their shorn hair? No, surely not. Beryl Hearnden
soon discovered that blast had blown two wigs out of a
shop window into a pool of blood.

However, clues had to be sifted minutely, painstakingly,
until there was no longer a doubt that every person in
the neighbourhood, including a stray passer-by, had been
accounted for. What had happened to Blondie of whom there
was no trace? Who last wore this torn piece of rose-coloured
material? How is it that no man ever seems to remember
how a woman is dressed? I asked Beryl Hearnden whether
these real-life experiences would change her technique in the
writing of detective stories, but she avoided giving me a
direct answer, saying that just then she was engaged as a
reader for a Hollywood film company. She read a great
number of modern novels every week in the hope of finding
stories suitable for the screen. The advantage of this work
was that she could do it at any time she pleased—even in
the middle of the night.

So strange had our manner of living become, that it did
not even strike her as incongruous to be discussing modern
novels between the task of finding an aged couple a new
home or driving some poor victim to the morgue.

Two days later on my way to Bond Street, I made a
detour by Selfridge's to see what had happened to the girls'
school. Had the pupils reassembled? No, they had been
given leave until 2nd January and the classroom in which
I had sat with the other women was now stacked with
salvaged furniture. One of the mistresses had adopted

a black cat which came to arch its back against my stockings, presumably out of general sense of gratitude for having been given a new home. By the time I reached Bond Street, though it was not yet five, the shops were all shut and the famous street practically deserted. Now and then a car would crawl through the fog, and one felt that the pulse of the city was beating more slowly.

The fog was densest near the park, and as night fell, American trucks would come to a standstill and the drivers jump out to inquire:

'Say, ma'am, are we near Piccadilly?'

'You're in it, soldier.'

'Thanks, lady.'

Pedestrians themselves formed convoys, led by those lucky enough to have electric torches. In the distance Big Ben, which had been out of order for a couple of days, was back at work, chiming:

> Lord, through this hour,
>   Be Thou our guide,
> That by Thy power
>   No foot shall slide,

before striking the hour.

CHRISTMAS Day was white, not with snow, but with hoar-frost which lay like a crisp carpet over the parks. The temperature, below zero, contracted the muscles of one's face and froze the puddles on the gravel walks. The sump, facing the Cornish elms in the Green Park drawing-room, had a coating of ice, and the roofs of the black huts studded round the big searchlight looked as if somebody had decorated them with sugar icing. A crimson sun low in the sky in the direction of Victoria was trying hard to penetrate the white mist that shrouded the wintry scene, and the searchlight, which was full on when I passed it, cast a bluish tint on the naked boughs of the maple trees screening

it from the deserted bandstand. Two soldiers were sawing
logs behind the cookhouse door, and from the courtyard
of Buckingham Palace came the strains of a military band
playing an old-fashioned waltz.

There were few people about—half a dozen American
soldiers and a woman exercising her poodle. The Mall was
quite deserted, and on one of the railings of the suspension
bridge which crossed the lake in St James's Park, I read
these words written in the frost: 'Doris Regina Rogers—
a happy Christmas.' Who was the girl with this regal name?
Had she been out walking early with a soldier friend who,
while bending over the bridge very close to her, had written
this message of love as he might have carved her initials on
the trunk of a beech tree? The towers of Westminster
Abbey, shrouded in mist, took on their medieval aspect,
powerful and mysterious. A taxi, its hood quite white, drew
up at the Abbey door, and I followed the occupants inside,
where a tall fir tree, decorated with coloured electric lights,
stood in front of the tomb of the Unknown Warrior, at the
four corners of which burned immense yellow candles whose
flames, bent by the draught, caused the wax to drip. The
scene of the Nativity against a coloured oriental backcloth
was softly lit. The nave was warm and wrapped in medita-
tion, and from afar came the voice of the preacher, himself
invisible until one had passed silently along the aisle past
the organ bridge.

Then one saw him in his white surplice and black stole
with a touch of crimson, venerably dignified and austere
against the ebony screen carved in front of the massive,
fluted and half-dim pillar of Normandy stone. All the candles
of the high altar were glimmering and flickering, shedding a
soft yellow and diffused light on fir trees, tapestry and gold
plate. The canon in residence, his head bowed, was seated
to the left of the communion table, and nearer to the pulpit
sat two vergers who by and by would escort the preacher
back to his place in the choir stalls. Just now his voice rose
and fell melodiously, while the vast congregation was so

hidden in shadow that one felt rather than perceived its presence.

The abbey was less filled with khaki than I had expected it to be, and yet I should have guessed that this would be so, for were not nearly all our troops of this theatre of war in Belgium and Holland, while the Americans were, at this very moment, engaged in the most bitter fighting since the invasion of the Continent?

For more than a week our thoughts had never left them. Anxiety had gripped us this Christmas, and Rundstedt's sudden and vicious attack had brought misery back to the liberated countries, threatening Liège, Sedan—even Brussels and Paris. Mentally we had reeled under the blow, and the holiday spirit had been singularly damped. We had thought more of the weather than of shopping. Had it not been for Bobby I would, in common with many other women, have dispensed with holly, mistletoe and pantomimes. The fog had hung dismally over London as it enshrouded the battle area. We had welcomed two bright days with a sudden lifting of our spirits, and never had we known greater cause to drop on our knees this Christmas morning to seek communion with our Maker.

A few hours after the first news of the breakthrough, Mme Brosselette arrived by air from the French capital to fetch her daughter Anne, who had completed the last term at Sherborne. Her arrival was no surprise because Anne had sent me her luggage from school, asking me to keep it until she was ready to go back with her mother to France. She spent the interval with a Polish school friend, placed in similar circumstances, with whom she came to see me one afternoon. She had become so attached to England and spoke English so fluently that she appeared genuinely sorry to be leaving.

Nobody understood better than her mother the spell of London. She quite changed after a few hours in its foggy streets and appeared overcome by nostalgia. During her two years' stay London had entwined its tentacles round her heart. She wore a trim, black suit, and her hair was gathered up at the back in a modest net. When the immigration officials at the English airport asked what her profession was, she answered simply, 'Member of Parliament', and they looked surprised. In fact, the Senate and Chamber of Deputies had both been dissolved, and these were replaced by a Consultative Assembly numbering two hundred and eighty, including twelve women of whom she was one. After lunch we went to Bond Street where she wished to buy a handbag for her daughter and a wallet for her son who was at college in Paris.

By New Year's Eve the fog had lifted, and though it was still bitterly cold the sky was full of stars, and a great white moon bathed the town in a milky glow that made the streets soft and mysterious. On such occasions our market had something old-fashioned about it, something almost medieval, with its quaint, narrow, winding alleys and small squat houses where an occasional lamp, shining through red curtains, with here and there a wisp of smoke curling up from a cracked chimney-pot, gave an impression of warmth and comfort within.

There was not a soul in sight, for the public-houses had been closed for nearly an hour, but in the distance one heard deep voices singing out of tune, and then they died away and there was silence. The cold was really intense, so dry and biting that when crossing St James's Park earlier in the evening I had noticed that the lake was frozen, with a few bricks and an old broom strewn on the surface, and there were notices dating from Victorian times warning Londoners not to put foot on the icy surface under penalty of a fine of five pounds, and that the wild fowl had disappeared from near the bridge, where they usually congregated, to seek refuge in the lee of the island on which stands the birdman's house. Everybody had stopped to look at the barometer facing the mulberry tree near St Anne's Gate, to read with a shiver of satisfaction that the temperature was well below freezing. Then they looked up at the clear sky and said: 'If our troops in the Ardennes have this sort of weather, everything will be well.' Already our worst fears had been relieved. Hourly the news, though scant, was better.

I was just enjoying the beauty of this wonderful night when there was a deafening roar, followed by a tremor, and every dog in the neighbourhood started to bark.

Piccadilly, with the Green Park stretching away in the distance, made such a splendid picture in the moonlight that I was glad to have come out. If this proved to be the last winter of the war, some of us would doubtless look back with a poet's eyes on the strange beauty of these nights. An American visitor had said: 'By day, London is greyer, more dirty, more battered than ever. But at night it becomes incredibly beautiful, in a way it will never be beautiful again. When all the lights go on once more, it will have the garishness of an ordinary city.' Already there were aspects of these wartime nights that we would not know again. Often Londoners, looking up in the moonlight at those silver balloons floating gently over the housetops, had exclaimed: 'What a lovely picture they make!' Others cried rapturously: 'They are our guardian angels. How we shall miss them after the war!' Yet, suddenly, during the battle of the flying bombs, they had all disappeared from the heart of London to form the gigantic barrage across the fields of Surrey and Kent, and now we had forgotten all about them. People said: 'The balloons? Why, I never even noticed they had gone!' It needed an effort to remember the beauty of that vast silver fleet riding gently at anchor, the swish of the wind in the cables and the strange encampments in our parks.

Of our own balloon in the Green Park no trace remained but a patch of yellowed grass and a vegetable garden run wild. The huts were demolished by a flying bomb. The

barbed wire was taken away with all the rest of the entangle-
ments towards the end of the summer. Curiously enough it
was one of the first balloons to make an appearance during
those far-off days when we pinned our faith on the Maginot
Line. When it went we were given splendid nocturnal
displays by the nearby searchlight, whose crew lived in a
house that might have come out of a fairy-tale. On a fine
night, when the stars shining above the naked boughs of
the poplars made them sparkle like illuminated Christmas
trees, this house in the woods was romantic.

On this New Year's Eve only a few cars passed along
Piccadilly. They all had one headlight on, a new concession
doing more than anything else to change the aspect of
London at night. A limousine drew up just ahead of me, and
I heard the chauffeur ask the way to a certain restaurant
where he was going to pick up some revellers. More and
more people, unable to find taxis, were using chauffeur-
driven hired cars to take them home after theatre or supper.
The garages which specialized in this work were open all
night, and their fleet of cars went from one assignment to the
other, for there was no scarcity of money.

Sounds of mild revelry came from the restaurant of the
Berkeley Hotel, and a few chinks of light were visible
through joins in the curtains. Very distantly the bells of
St Martin-in-the-Fields pealed in the New Year. A bottle
of whisky fell from a sailor's unsteady hands into the roadway. Voices struck up 'Auld Lang Syne'.

1945

1945

I HAD, of course, received no news of my little farm in Normandy, the house in which Bobby was born, the house I had left at such short notice that the uneaten lunch lay still warm on the kitchen table. My mother, as I have already said, was in Versailles. An American officer, a friend of Mrs Dorothy Berker, had succeeded in reaching her, taking her provisions and news that we in London were still alive. She had thought about us, and especially about her little grandson, all through those terrible years, just as I had suffered indescribable mental torture worrying about her, blaming myself, my husband, for being obliged to leave her without resources on the quayside at St Malo.

Every morning the postman used to push the letters through the flap in the front door of our apartment at Carrington House, and as soon as this happened, Bobby would rush into the tiny hall to pick them up and bring them to me.

One morning in the early spring he brought me a postcard which in his eyes appeared so dull that, as he handed it to me, he said with a disappointed air: 'Mother, look! This is all the postman brought this morning!'

Though he could not guess it, he was bearing in his hands a message of joy. Dr Lehérissey, the doctor who had brought him into the world, was giving us the news we had been so eagerly waiting for. I seized the thin card with its two postage stamps, the one showing the head of Marshal Pétain, the other depicting the Arc de Triomphe, and this was what I read:

Our village, saved by a miracle from the desolation all

253

round us, is intact except for that part of it nearest the
railway station. Your house is still standing, though
emptied of all its contents. I hope that as soon as these
emotions have calmed down a little, we shall have the
pleasure of seeing you again, and I pray you to kiss
most affectionately on my behalf your son who must by
now have become a big boy,

Dr Lehérissey.

AFTER a cold, damp Easter, the weather turned very warm,
and by mid April a temperature of eighty-two in the shade
was recorded in Regent Street. The Rhine had been crossed,
the Allied armies were swarming over Germany, and with
the last V-sites in Holland cleared, the siege of London was
finally raised.

Those terrifying thuds which for so long had broken
the stillness of the night or had rumbled over the roar of
traffic during the hours of daylight, causing pinched faces
suddenly to turn a little whiter, ceased for twelve hours,
twenty-four hours . . . and then disappeared from our lives.
Londoners found it difficult to believe that the long battle
had come to an end. But as each peaceful night gave way
to a peaceful day, as each bout of hot sunshine hastened the
unfolding of the lilac, brightened the beds of St James's
Park with multi-coloured tulips, and covered the boughs
of tardy oak and ash with tender leaves, they began to
relax and feel that a new energy was surging in their veins,
like the sap of spring.

London was crowded, London was picturesque and full
of expectancy. The great cities of Germany were falling
into our hands; men who had been in prison camps since
Dunkirk were being freed; and from Magdeburg and
Kustrin the pincers were closing on the heart of the Reich.

The sudden death of President Roosevelt became known
in London one morning when the sun had risen trium-
phantly on its course—moving contrast between sunshine

and sorrow. The passing, at the approach of victorious peace, of the man who had believed in us during the dark days of the battle of Britain was indeed poignant. The flags that fluttered at half-mast in the heat haze high above Piccadilly; the genuine consternation on the faces of the American military police who lined up in the Green Park that Saturday morning to parade under the black-crêped Stars and Stripes; the realization that there would be no more of those meetings of the Big Three, dimmed the sun but could not hide it.

Events were moving so fast that Londoners were dazed. They listened night and morning to the mighty, incessant throb of bombers thundering to Germany. Never had such armadas passed over London. They flew above the rooftops and in the blue night the victory signals flashed like stars. By the light of dawn, while the air was still rent by the noise, four fine bays were drawing a practice brake from Buckingham Palace to St Paul's Cathedral, outriders in plain livery riding in front. This was the rehearsal for the King's drive through his victorious capital. Then, perhaps, sweat and blood, misery and oppression, sleepless months, separation and anguish would be nightmares of the past.